Nav
the Clickety-Clack

NAVIGATING THE CLICKETY-CLACK

How to Live a Peace-Filled Life in a Seemingly Toxic World
Volume 4

Featuring:
Bob Doyle, Marci Shimoff, and Rickie Byars

Also Featuring:
Contributing Authors—Rachel Ann, Patti-Jane (PJ) Ashley,
Claire Chitty, Lottie Cooper, Heather Davis, Sally Estlin, Nadine Felix,
Maureen Marhayla, Nami Nesterowicz, Nevaeh Pillsbury,
Lisa Jeanine Ramirez, Dipal Shah, Jenny Stapleton,
DL Walker, and Renee Zukin

BEYOND
BELIEF
—PUBLISHING—
YOU HOLD THE FUTURE IN YOUR HANDS

Rev. Michael Beckwith / Fletch Rainey

This book is dedicated to our dear friend and spiritual mentor, Fletch Rainey. RIP, dear Fletch. May your teachings about the Clickety-Clack live on and serve humanity for many years to come.

Praise for
Navigating the Clickety-Clack
Volume 4

"*Navigating the Clickety-Clack* is a must-read if you're looking to create peace and calm within your life."

—John Coote
CEO of Wellness Leadership Academy

"*Navigating the Clickety-Clack* shares the gift of alignment wisdom when it is needed most on the planet."

—Bridget Quigg
Founder of *You're a Genius* workshop series

"A fantastic, uplifting book by teachers who speak the hidden truths of the universe."

—Joan Posivy, Bestselling Author of
The Way Success Works:
How to Decide, Believe, and Begin to Live Your Best Life

"I loved *Navigating the Clickety-Clack*. What I liked most was the blueprint the authors provided for getting through the myriad of self-talk that keeps all of us from reaching our potential. I didn't even realize I was automatically thinking some of these things. Great book; wonderful info!"

—S.H. Bown
Author, *The House of Roga* trilogy

"Living a peace-filled life during this time in history is no easy task. *Navigating the Clickety-Clack* gives us many tools from a wide variety of experienced voices."

—Tasha Chen
Vision and Mind Mastery Mentor

"As a Naturopathic Doctor and Stress Reset Expert, I help stressed and burned-out women with adrenal fatigue improve their mood, balance their hormones, and increase their energy. *Navigating the Clickety-Clack* is a goldmine that can help my clients get there faster!"

—Dr. Erin Kinney

"No words can describe how important this book is in today's ever-changing chaos and confusion. Highly sensitive and empathic people need ways to stay calm and centered in order to shine their light. *Navigating the Clickety-Clack* is a wisdom-filled book that shows you how.

—Mary Perry
Spiritual Healer and Seraphim Blueprint Teacher

"As a Soulcologist and Soul Purpose Mentor, I've had the privilege of working with beautiful, sensitive entrepreneurial women from around the globe. Being able to be calm in the eye of the storm is essential to tapping into your Soul's intuition. I highly recommend *Navigating the Clickety-Clack* for all the amazing tools it offers in this space!"

—Kimberley Banfield
Founder of Soulcology

"This book is right on time. If ever there was a time to have the gift of neutrality, it's now."

—A.J. Ali, Director and Producer
of the film, *Walking While Black: L.O.V.E. Is The Answer*

"The message of *Navigating the Clickety-Clack* is this: It's not what happens to you but how you react to it that matters. I highly recommend this wonderful, insightful book, which is so needed for these challenging times!"

—Lisa Winston, host of *The Mindset Reset Show*
#1 Bestselling Author, Speaker, and Coach
MindsetResetTV.com

"*Navigating the Clickety-Clack* provides concrete steps to make positive changes in your emotional and spiritual health and to build a remarkably happy personal life experience."

—Bethany Sharifi, Writer

"*Navigating the Clickety-Clack* provides easy-to-follow steps, allowing you to learn how to make positive changes in your emotional and spiritual health. This book is a must-read."

—Keith Vitali
Actor, Martial Artist, Writer, Movie Producer

"As an international Wellness Expert, I'm always on the lookout for practical, actionable advice to help my clients live and enjoy a healthier life. *Navigating the Clickety-Clack* is a book whose time has come. We could all use more peace and joy in our lives, especially now. Highly recommend!"

—DL Walker, MSEd, PT
Founder of Correcticise Your Life and Fixuonline.com

"As an Integrative Health Specialist, I understand the significance of moving through trauma to discover total health. *Navigating the Clickety-Clack* is the perfect companion to the integrative health practices I teach my clients. This is a must-read for anyone seeking to find calm in the chaos."

—Keli Jones
Integrative Health Specialist

"Sometimes living in the unknown is uncomfortable. This book will support you to navigate those times with grace and ease."

—Theresa Coates Ellis
City Councilwoman of Manassas, Virginia

"Inspirational, uplifting, and heartwarming stories that help reconnect us all back to our inner strength and innate power."

—Bruce Langford
Host of top-ranked podcast *Mindfulness Mode*

"It's often through challenging times that we learn just how strong we really are and that we can overcome anything."

—Leslie Welch, CDC Certified Divorce Coach,
Career Coach, and Life Coach

"This is the kind of book that makes you stop in your tracks and look up from the text as you realize the power of a new perspective on what is. It empowers us to pedal through the Clickety-Clack we all face, every day. Brilliant."

—Bryan Falchuk, CPT BCS, three-time TEDx Speaker,
and Bestselling Author of *Do a Day*

"I am passionate about helping my clients design extraordinary lives in their Third Act. This book holds deep insight to navigating that major life change with clarity, confidence, and courage!"

—Denise Peterson
Intentional Life Change Expert

"If you have finished living a life of anger and frustration, and you're looking for a way to build a life filled with peace and joy, this is the book for you."

—Melody Chadamoyo
Author, Relationship and Law of Attraction Coach

Contents

Acknowledgments 13

Introduction 15

Bob Doyle 19

Marci Shimoff 25

Rickie Byars 33

Rachel Ann 39

Patti-Jane (PJ) Ashley 43

Claire Chitty 49

Lottie Cooper 57

Heather Davis 65

Sally Estlin 75

Nadine Felix 83

Maureen Marhayla 93

Nami Nesterowicz 101

Nevaeh Pillsbury 107

Lisa Jeanine Ramirez 113

Dipal Shah 119

Jenny Stapleton 125

DL Walker 133

Renee Zukin 139

Conclusion 147

About the Publisher 149

Acknowledgments

It is with deep appreciation that I thank all the authors who said YES to participating in this powerful project.

Thanks to Bob Proctor, Jack Canfield, Christy Whitman, Marie Diamond, Adam Markel, Joe Vitale, Michael Beckwith, Marci Shimoff, Bob Doyle, Rickie Byars, and John Demartini for being such great mentors and for always saying yes. Your support over the years has been instrumental in our success as authors and publishers.

Thank you to our incredible team who brought this book forward to completion and to the world one step at a time: Karen Burton, Heather Taylor, Bethany Knowles, Barbara Strnadova, Autumn Carlton, MaryDes, Rudy Milanovich, and Pam Murphy.

Thank you to all the teachers, speakers, and thought leaders who provided the tips, tools, and workshops that taught all the master teachers in this book how to stay peaceful, even during the Clickety-Clack of everyday life.

Introduction

Hello. My name is Keith Leon S., owner of Beyond Belief Publishing, and I want to welcome you to our book designed to help you in *Navigating the Clickety-Clack*. As we begin this journey together, you may not yet understand the title, but I am confident you navigate this troubling place from time to time. We all do.

Back in 2005, my wife, Maura, and I met a man named Fletch Rainey at the Agape International Center of Truth in California. We became good friends with Fletch. Eventually, he created a group called "The Spiritual Posse" and became one of our spiritual mentors. We would reach out to him when we were freaking out about money, business challenges, and fears or when we were in flux, not knowing what to do next.

One time when we called him with one of our issues, he said, "Relax, you are just in the Clickety-Clack."

We asked, "What is the Clickety-Clack?"

Fletch said, "Remember when you had a ten-speed bicycle, and you changed from one gear to another? There is that moment when the chain is jumping from one gear to the next gear, but it has not clicked in yet. What sound does it make? *Clickety-Clack . . . Clickety-Clack.* You have faith it will catch eventually, so you keep peddling the bike. Your faith pays off because it eventually catches, and when it does, you are off into an even better gear. That is where you are right now—you are in the Clickety-Clack. Have faith and know that things will kick in to the next gear soon enough. Trust, and know that all is well."

His reply would stay with us. To this day, when Maura and I are experiencing worry or not knowing what to do next, one of us will look at the other and say, "Clickety-Clack." Other times I have experienced the Clickety-Clack are when others around me are freaking out, coming unglued, or being judgmental, hateful, or angry toward me.

In a world filled with so much anger, resentment, judgment, hate, shame, and finger-pointing, how is one supposed to stay peaceful?

Over the years, I have developed tools to remain calm and peaceful in these times. People have asked me how I am able to do this. The answer is multi-layered, and it has taken me years to arrive at this point.

Here are some practices that have helped me over the years:

- Experiential growth workshops
- *The Work* of Byron Katie
- Prayer and meditation
- Teachings from the mystics
- Minding my thoughts and language

In the spring of 2020, the COVID-19 pandemic kept us all in our homes. This was a time of inner reflection for me. I took time to go within and look for answers to the question: *What's next for me?* I had visions of our dear friend Fletch and his teaching us about the Clickety-Clack. I thought: *If ever there were a time to stay calm and peaceful, it's now.*

With so much seemingly toxic information, news, and energy around us, wouldn't now be a great time to gain some tools for neutrality? I thought to myself: *I know people who are living these principles every day. I am friends with people who are able to stay peaceful, even now.* This thought led me to reach out to three dear friends and mentors: Bob Proctor, Jack Canfield, and Christy Whitman. I shared the title and subtitle with them, and they said they would love to participate in this book.

Next, I made a short list of other friends I knew who were walking and talking demonstrations of staying peaceful when others were not able to do so. I contacted these friends and asked them if they would like to participate. At the end of each call, I asked each friend, "Do you know someone who is living a peace-filled life in a seemingly toxic world?" The people they recommended appear in these pages. It is important to me that every person in this book lives this principle.

Each person in this book is living what they will share and teach you!

In your hands is the fourth book of the series. The first three books were award-winning international bestsellers and have supported readers through turbulent times. The public keeps asking for more, and we're happy to continue bringing forth experts to share their stories and tools with you. I extend my thanks to Bob Doyle, Marci Shimoff, and Rickie Byars for their contributions to this fourth volume.

I suggest taking your time reading this book. Read one story at a time, then stop and meditate on what was shared. Take notes, write in a journal, and decide if there is a next step you would like to take, such as researching teachers, programs, or seminars recommended.

I have put together for you the finest group of people to share their Clickety-Clack stories, how they navigated out of the Clickety-Clack, and how they are able to stay peaceful inside, no matter what is happening outside. May you enjoy each and every word. May you be guided to the next steps and ultimately discover what is called *the peace that passes all understanding.*

Bob Doyle

How has the Clickety-Clack shown up in your life?

I have had several significant transition periods in my life that involved a lot of Clickety-Clack. Probably the most notable is the one that moved me into teaching the Law of Attraction or the business of transformation in general. I quit my corporate job and had absolutely no safety net whatsoever except a lot of faith that something was going to happen. In the time after quitting my job, I created my first program, called *Create Your Reality*.

Those months were a tough ride because I was still studying the concept I was teaching. I was not experiencing a lot of success. All the little things I was putting together to make money were not working, including programs about manifesting. I was speaking before I had the experience, which a lot of people in our industry do. I was one of those people, so clearly that did not work for me.

I made a lot of adjustments because money was running out. It was the classic situation in which creditors were calling, and it was not looking good. That transition period feels like it was one of the highest impact areas of the Clickety-Clack in my life.

How did you navigate the Clickety-Clack?

One of my early distinctions in this whole transformation conversation was to get out of my head. I needed to let go and follow my intuition. I had been trying to *figure out* what was wrong, so all my attention was focused on the problem I was trying to solve. None of my intellect or experience or technical ability was changing any of that as a reality. I was still struggling, and nothing was working.

I came to realize that I needed to let go and trust and create a vision of what I truly wanted my life to be. I needed to stop trying to fix problems and, instead, to gain clarity by asking myself these questions: *How do I want things to look? Who do I want to be?*

That was my first real exercise in following and trusting my intuition in a major way. I did not have any experience of doing that, so I wasn't sure how I was going to show up. I made a decision for myself: *Okay, I am going to hold this vision of what I want my life to be. I am going to stop looking at what it isn't and focus on who I want to be, how I want my life to be. Then, I am going to see what shows up in life that is out of the ordinary—something I didn't calculate, strategize, or try to make happen.*

Next, I had this chance unusual conversation about angels at a networking event where I felt completely out of place. I am not an angel person, but I began following the suggestions from this person. I couldn't tell you much about who the angels were, but I was receiving signs to follow. I was having fun and started seeing angels.

In retrospect, my reticular activating system was in full-on angel mode, so I was going to see the angels. Following these promptings led me to a bookstore, which led me to an event I held, which led me to a person I met, which led me to a book. That book was called *A Happy Pocket Full of Money* and was written by David Cameron Gikandi (2008). That book turned on all the lights for me in terms of the science of manifesting and wealth consciousness. His words filled in the blanks left by all the metaphysical stuff, the more woo-woo kind of conversations that my brain—while wanting to believe and accept—was having a hard time accepting.

After reading that book, things happened fast. I started to implement some of the practices I read with a newfound understanding of why these things would work. It was basic Law of Attraction stuff, like changing the background wallpaper on my computer, using it as a vision board. I started seeing results. Things were clearly shifting in my life, and that's when I put together the first *Wealth Beyond Reason* Program.

I had built a network of people online by creating a conversation of physique transformation. It wasn't making me any money, but it was a passion at the time, and it gave me my first community. When I told them about the new direction I was going and why I was so excited about it, they were my first round of customers. They bought the first program; then it grew by word of mouth, and it grew into this monster.

So, that all came about from letting go of trying to figure it out and just allowing the Universe to show me the way. This was a whole new experience for me. Sure, I felt foolish a few times as I learned how to present this new information, but, ultimately, it led me exactly where I needed to be.

What tools do you recommend for staying peaceful in a seemingly toxic world?

I wish back then I had the set of tools I have now. If I had to choose just one tool, it would be breathwork. I would advise everybody to learn a handful of breathwork techniques because they directly affect your physiology.

You see, a lot of the things that make us feel bad and lead us to make wrong decisions are simply part of our wiring. This subject is the predominant conversation I have now: how we have been wired, when we have a reaction, and how our whole body comes into play. We need to interrupt these patterns, not just mentally, but also physically.

Learning various breathwork techniques can, in just a few moments, completely change not just your mental state, but your physiological state as well. Breathing techniques can turn down the cortisol and shut off the stories you automatically tell—replacing them with wonderful silence. Breathwork is my number one go-to because you can do it anywhere, anytime. There are so many techniques available to us, and they are all amazing.

About the Author

Bob Doyle is best known as a Law of Attraction Expert, featured in the film and book *The Secret*. Bob is driven by his passion for creative self-expression and has been coaching people through the process of becoming their ideal selves for over twenty years. He recently turned his attention to *neuroplasticity*, the ability to change our brain, realizing that our reality and our quality of life are governed by the wiring of our brain and how we process our everyday experiences. Bob is the creator of the *Evolve Your Excellence* brain rewiring program, as well as a certified breathwork instructor. He combines multiple modalities into a simple process of lasting transformation.

Find out more at: EvolveYourExcellence.com.

Marci Shimoff

How has the Clickety-Clack shown up in your life?

Every time I have moved to another level in my life that involved success, it has always been preceded by the Clickety-Clack. That includes when I was teaching to rooms of twenty and thirty people, and I knew I was supposed to teach to thousands, but it was not happening yet. Then, the *Chicken Soup for the Woman's Soul* series happened for me and moved me to another level. That was one time the Clickety-Clack showed up.

But I want to talk more about the time after that. I felt very blessed to be able to co-author the women's books in the *Chicken Soup for the Soul* series. I wrote seven books in this series, and they sold millions of copies. I loved doing it. I did that for about seven years, and then I realized I had cooked up all the *Chicken Soup* that I could possibly cook. I was done.

It was as if the energy of that life chapter was over, and I knew I wanted to do something else. I was inspired to write a book on being happy, because even though I had great success with the *Chicken Soup for the Woman's Soul* books, I still did not feel deeply happy.

But how do you walk away from something that is already going so well to follow your heart? That was hard.

The Clickety-Clack came in so many ways. People said to me, "You cannot possibly stop. You must keep on doing this."

This feedback made it difficult for me to stay true to myself, to go deep inside and ask: *What do I want to do?* But I did and transitioned from a very active stage of life to a more inward stage while I was coming up with everything I needed for *Happy for No Reason.*

Let me share a quick story. When I came up with the idea of the specialty books *Chicken Soup for the Woman's Soul* series back in 1995, I was on a seven-day silent meditation retreat. In the middle of a meditation, a light bulb went off in my head. I saw the words, CHICKEN SOUP FOR THE WOMAN'S SOUL, and I knew what I was supposed to do. At the time, the only book that was out was the original *Chicken Soup for the Soul* book. So, I called my mentor, Jack Canfield, the originator of the series, and I shared my idea.

He said, "Oh my God, that is such a great idea."

And the rest is history.

It took my going away on a silent seven-day meditation retreat to come up with that idea. The idea of *Chicken Soup for the Woman's Soul* came on the fourth day. So, when it was time to write about happiness, and I couldn't come up with the title, I thought: *Remember what happened when I went away in silence and came up with the idea for Chicken Soup? I'll do the same thing, but I will do just four days of silence instead of seven, because that is all I needed the first time to come up with the Chicken Soup for the Woman's Soul idea.*

Sure enough, I went away on a four-day silent retreat, and on the morning of the fourth day, the title *Happy for No Reason* came to me. I had already been through about two hundred titles and knew that none of them were right. But this title came to me in the same way that the *Chicken Soup for the Woman's Soul* idea did, out of that silence. That was part of the process of birthing.

In the Clickety-Clack, you are in the unknown, and you have to be okay with being uncomfortable. You have to be okay with living in the questions of *What do I do?* or *What is next?* It is almost always through some kind of silence or inward dive that ideas are generated for what is next in the outer aspect of life.

How did you navigate the Clickety-Clack?

I once learned from a wise teacher that our lives go through cycles of rest and activity. When I was writing the *Chicken Soup for the Woman's Soul* books, I had been in tremendous activity. I knew that I needed to retreat and take time to go inside for the rest cycle so the next cycle of activity could be powerful.

I shifted into a more inward time. I meditated regularly, which I do all the time. But additionally, I took a meditation retreat.

I also had a women's mastermind support group, and I opened up for them to support me during this time of the unknown. When I started thinking: *Oh that is it! I will never do anything else with my life. I am a one-hit wonder with Chicken Soup, and that is the end of my career,* they would encourage me.

They would say, "No, there's more. Stick with it and follow your heart. Do not look at the outside appearances of what is happening or not happening but stay aligned with what you know to be right."

I listened to them and used every known tool to stay true to my heart in every moment. I would practice EFT tapping when I would start to feel self-doubt, or sometimes I would use the Sedona Method, or *The Work* of Byron Katie. I tried many different practices based on whatever need I felt at the moment.

Most importantly, I stayed in the space, in the zone of believing in myself.

What tools do you recommend for staying peaceful in a seemingly toxic world?

The average person has sixty thousand thoughts a day, and for the average person, 80 percent of those are negative. This tendency is called the *negativity bias*. We inherited this from our prehistoric ancestors.

A *negativity bias* means we have a propensity to focus on the negative, to notice the negative. The happiest and most successful people I have witnessed reverse that tendency. They create a tendency for the positive, to notice the positive, to savor the positive. So, we need to create new neuropathways in the brain for the positive. And we can do that with three simple steps.

The first step is to *be on the lookout for the good*. One idea is to imagine you are a member of the Academy Awards committee and your job is to give out awards every day. For example: You might give out the Cutest Dog of the Day award. Or, the Kindest Act of the Day award. Mentally hand out Academy Awards all day.

The second step is to *savor the good* for at least twenty seconds. It takes that long for the good to register in your brain enough to start to create new neuropathways for the positive.

And the third step is to *aim for a three-to-one ratio*—find three positives for every negative.

Regularly practicing these three simple steps can help bring more peace and happiness to your world.

You could also adopt the simple practice that I learned from the Institute of Heartmath, called the *Inner Ease technique*. It takes just a moment to do, but it helps shift you into what is called Heart Rhythm Coherence, which helps you open your heart to more love.

Who doesn't need more of that these days?

You can do the Inner Ease Technique with your eyes open or closed. Start by putting your hand on your heart, bringing your attention there. Then, begin *heart-focused breathing*. Imagine you are breathing in and out through the center of your heart. Do that for a minute or so in nice, slow, rhythmic breaths. Then with each breath, bring into your heart feelings of love, ease, and compassion.

To encourage these feelings, you might think of someone who helps you feel that way. Or, you can remember the last time you felt love, ease, and compassion. Or, you can silently say the words to yourself: *love, ease,* and *compassion.* If you do this practice a few minutes, two or three times a day for the next few weeks, you will be more and more in the habit of Heart Rhythm Coherence, which will bring more peace.

It is now more important than ever that we each stay in peace. If each one of us experiences greater peace, not only do we generate more creativity and happiness in our own lives, but we spread both gifts to everyone around us.

About the Author

Marci Shimoff is a #1 *New York Times* bestselling author, a world-renowned transformational teacher, and an expert on happiness, success, and unconditional love. Her books include the international bestsellers *Happy for No Reason* and *Love for No Reason.* Marci is also the woman's face of the biggest self-help book phenomenon in history as co-author of six books in the *Chicken Soup for the Woman's Soul* series. With total book sales of more than sixteen million copies worldwide in thirty-three languages, Marci is one of the bestselling female nonfiction authors of all time.

Marci is also a featured teacher in the international film and book sensation, *The Secret,* and **the host of the PBS TV show,** *Happy for No Reason.* She narrated the award-winning movie *Happy.*

Marci delivers keynote addresses and seminars on happiness, success, empowerment, and unconditional love to Fortune 500 companies, professional and nonprofit organizations, women's associations, and audiences around the world.

Marci is currently leading a one-year mentoring program called *Your Year of Miracles.* Her opening seminar has been heard by more than 200,000 people.

Marci earned her MBA from UCLA and holds an advanced certificate as a stress management consultant. She is a founding member and on the board of directors of the Transformational Leadership Council, a group of 100 top transformational leaders.

Through her books and her presentations, Marci's message has touched the hearts and rekindled the spirits of millions of people throughout the world. She is dedicated to helping people live more empowered and joy-filled lives.

To learn more about Marci, please visit her website at: HappyForNoReason.com or MarciShimoff.com.

Rickie Byars

How has the Clickety-Clack shown up in your life?

The Clickety-Clack has shown up in my life across the board. Apparently, part of my journey to becoming the person I came here to be included learning how to adjust in the middle of complete chaos—how to find my bearings, how to maintain, even when I could see nothing stable around me.

For example, in my early twenties I went to New York, looking to get a record deal with Stevie Wonder. I was encouraged to go to New York by my spouse. One very challenging day, I said, "This marriage is over. It ain't working, and we shouldn't have done it the way we did. Anyway, I am out of here."

He replied, "No, no, you are just having a bad day. What you need to do is go to New York, find Stevie Wonder, and get your record deal."

I was living in Atlanta, Georgia, and that sounded like a plan. How naive I was! But I was willing to do what was needed in order to hit the mark I had set for myself.

I called my older brother Xavier, and he said, "Come on, Sis!" He said he had a place for me, and he invited me to stay with him and his family in their apartment in Brooklyn. I took that step without knowing anything; I just stepped out in faith into New York City.

One thing led to another. I had just one connection. I had the Stevie Wonder publishing company address, Black Bull Publishing. I imagined that Stevie loved the cassette I had given to him, and all I wanted was to talk about a record deal. I was so excited. So there I was.

One thing led to another, and I got an appointment. When I went to the office, they said Stevie wasn't there, but his brother had a little time for me. He was blunt in his questions, his response, and his reactions to my questions. I was looking for the demo cassette I had given to Stevie. I wanted to know how Stevie felt about my music, and this man said, "Your cassette could be in a trunk in Detroit."

I had a name: John Harris. John Harris was Stevie's road manager, and he had told me to keep in touch. I was told that John Harris was on the road. This guy was real with me, but it felt unreal.

How did you navigate the Clickety-Clack?

I walked out the door. I had nothing. I had come all the way from Atlanta, with a pleather coat, in the middle of winter, to see Stevie Wonder and make a record deal—to meet someone who could help me. In that moment, I stood in the Clickety-Clack.

I stood in the hallway. I won't say I was devastated, but I was quite disappointed. Then, a woman in the hallway was going to the restroom. When she walked by, I asked her, "Do you work at Columbia Records?"

She said, "I am going to the restroom, I will be right back."

When she came back, I asked her again if she worked at Columbia Records, and she said, "No, but I have friends who do. I am just doing some work here. And Columbia Records is just down the hallway."

I did not know that. I said, "I have a cassette. Would you listen to this and give this to the A and R (artists and repertoire) person there, if you know somebody?"

This lady took all my information. She said, "Where are you from?" I told her, and she said "I like you. Thank you for giving me this, and I look forward to hearing your music. I will get back to you."

In that moment, I was flying by the seat of my faith because nothing had turned out like I thought it would. Sure enough, within a week, I got a phone call from this lady, and she said "Guess what? I set up an appointment with somebody at Warner Brothers and her name is Donna Halpern. She is not the A and R director, but she is the interim person. She wants to talk to you."

I went to see her. One thing led to another, and in three weeks' time, I did have my record deal. It wasn't with Stevie Wonder; it was with Muse Records, a prestigious little jazz label that still produces incredible jazz recordings.

I was an unknown songwriter from Atlanta, Georgia, who came with a plan I thought made sense. When I got there, it was as if life said to me: *This ain't no plan, girl.*

I replied: *What is your plan?* Apparently, the plan was to connect to the first person who was willing to listen to what I had.

What tools do you recommend for staying peaceful in a seemingly toxic world?

The first tool is to learn how to breathe. We have to learn how to breathe because some things take our breath away—and not in a good way.

Learn how to breathe, and learn to watch what is going on. Take everything in and then take time to understand what it means and how best to respond as who you truly are.

I am testing those tools right now because life has been strange. My whole incarnation has been strange. The world did not become toxic yesterday, you know. America has been kind of sick. There has been a toxicity in this country that began long before I was born—not this continent, but this country.

The way that I have navigated all the chaos has been through breathing. Breathing helps me stop. It helps me see how best to be in any scenario because what is happening on the other side of the world is also happening right here, right now.

After I stop, I observe it all and respond as best I can from all I am, and that includes what I can do. I offer it to God. I allow God to carry me and to guide me. And I give thanks for what I can do and even more for what I can be.

About the Author

Rickie Byars is an acclaimed and beloved singer-songwriter in the genre of Inspirational/New Thought music. Her music resonates in churches of all denominations throughout the world. Live audiences and YouTube streamers who take part in her weekly B-hood Sunday devotionals are uplifted through her music and her messages—always delivered with joy and sincerity. She has created an inspirational twenty-four-hour radio station, Bradio.org, which blasts beautiful songs from her golden era at the Agape International Spiritual Center where Rickie was the founding Choir Director for thirty years and Music and Arts Director for many years. Rickie has released nine solo albums of inspirational music and has produced seven choral music albums, three songbooks, and two volumes of choral music arrangements. She even found the time to write a mini-memoir about her illustrious career.

Rickie cares deeply about her community. In 2009, with a team of intergenerational artists, she established Kuumba in Motion, a nonprofit inspirational initiative that empowers individuals to discover their inherent gifts and talents through exposure to nature, the arts, and creative sciences. For twenty-four years, Rickie cofacilitated the Soul Sisters women's retreats, empowering women through workshops, meditations, and various healing modalities. She sits on the board of directors of Voices4Freedom.org, an abolitionist organization working to free enslaved children, women, and men in northern India. Rickie inspires all to do better and be better.

Find out more at: RickieByars.org.

Rachel Ann

How has the Clickety-Clack shown up in your life?

The Clickety-Clack has shown up in my life through my brother's death, which set the whole world on fire for my family and me. His death brought back all prior deaths. Then, after my brother's death, my aunt was murdered. There was a lot of Clickety-Clack space surrounding that one death.

After my brother died, my mother decided to reveal to me that my father was not my biological father. I had been suspicious throughout my whole life as I compared my looks to my siblings', my dad's toenails to my toenails—everything you can imagine. I had asked them outright if he was my dad.

They replied, "Oh, that's ridiculous Rachel."

Finally, I put it to rest, but I still was uncertain about it. My mom was a mess after my brother died, so she told me that my dad was not my dad.

The Clickety-Clack came again not even six weeks after my brother's death, when my son decided to tell me he thought he had found my biological father. My thoughts raced: *What? What? I did not ask you to do that.*

I was in a bit of a spiral from all three of these things happening in a short time. My world as I knew it changed completely after those events took place.

How did you navigate the Clickety-Clack?

All these things made me stop. When my brother died, it was unexpected. Not only did I stop, but my whole entire family stopped—our whole life completely stopped. It made me realize how extremely connected I was to my family, yet it also made me realize how traumatized I was as a result of being so connected to them. I was forced to start learning about the gifts I had carried my whole life without realizing them. It opened my eyes, as I went back to my childhood and reopened the gifts I had as a child in God, in Spirit.

I became hungry—hungry to know more about myself, to uncover myself. I learned all kinds of modalities of healing from various teachers, and I found gratitude in the chaos. I even found gratitude and connections from past traumas.

For instance, I found that my mom treated me the way she did because of her own traumas. I was able to see other people's footsteps, how other people walked their lives. I came to understand what they had gone through and why I had to experience what I had experienced. I understood that events in my life had brought me to that crucial point, allowing me to take that stop, that pause.

I also navigated through *surrender*. Once I learned these things happened for a reason, I was able to surrender and allow the process to happen. I was able to step into being a witness, to watch and almost become a scientist as I unraveled these happenings.

I brought it all to a place of connection—to see connections and patterns—and was able to understand why things had to happen as they did.

I realized I am not in control; there is something at work much bigger than me. I began to redesign my life.

What tools do you recommend for staying peaceful in a seemingly toxic world?

I recommend breathing and meditating in any moment of *Now*, knowing you can reset. It is always Now, always Now.

I recommend viewing life from a point of being a witness, from a child's perspective. Find the awe. Find the beauty in everything, even in the things perceived as trauma or tragedy. It is there. You can find it.

Go out into nature. First, you might need to find your pause moment before you can become a witness. My favorite thing to do is go into nature to unplug and get away from the norm, away from the everyday world and the societal norm. Go into nature and start witnessing how nature is so interconnected—how all the animals and bugs interact with the mycelium and the trees. It is *all* connected.

Then, you can realize how you are also connected.

My number one suggestion is to let go, just let go and breathe. Stop. Breathe. Remember that you are not in control. Then, you can step back into the flow and witness it. You will really feel the difference when you step into it again.

About the Author

Rachel Ann is an adventurer in self-discovery. She has a deep passion for searching out *truth*; in particular, Divine truth. Her thirst for life, combined with her passion to seek and explore, allows her to share great tools with her clientele that they may use in their own self-discovery, including energy healing, shamanic studies, indigenous customs, yogic teachings, and psychic mediumship. She desires to share these treasures in hopes of helping others find the tools they need to uncover their truest selves, thus creating a much more peaceful version of this world that we share together. Rachel has an inner knowing that guides her through this lifetime.

Rachel is the founder and CEO of Adventures in Self-Discovery and is a yoga instructor, Reiki master, IET practitioner, and student of shamanic methods. She conducts private sessions and travels to lead retreats and workshops.

She invites others to discover what it takes to fulfill their deepest desires. She advocates uniting mind, body, and spirit. She may be contacted at rachel-ann.com.

Patti-Jane (PJ) Ashley

How has the Clickety-Clack shown up in your life?

The Clickety-Clack shows up when multiple deadlines clash, and we come to a point in my organization where it is impossible to continue. This situation creates a lot of stress for me, my organization, and the team. It feels like a locomotive train with a mind of its own, going out of control, faster and faster and impossible to stop.

The stress creates a burden on my organization and me until something has to give. That *giving* is usually me. As a team, we then examine all the competing issues and our priorities and ask: *How do we get through this? How do we stick with our mission and our priorities?*

It's as if the Clickety-Clack takes over the organization and me, having a mind of its own. It speeds up the pace, making it hard to identify once you are in it. Generally, something needs to give or break for me to recognize that I am back in it again, into that Clickety-Clack. Once I accept that it's back, then I know what to do about it.

How did you navigate the Clickety-Clack?

In my case, the Clickety-Clack presents itself quite often. The first thing needed is acceptance that it is actually happening. With that acceptance comes the understanding that I need to find a remedy for the situation. Without acceptance, the Clickety-Clack keeps going and going and going.

Acceptance is the first point in navigating it. Once I accept it, calmness returns to my journey.

Second, then, is *awareness*. After acceptance, I need to be aware of what it is doing to me, my team, our practitioners, and our clients—closely looking at the organization, our mental health, and our physical energy. I ask: *How is the Clickety-Clack presenting?* The more we are aware of how it shows up in our business, the quicker we can see and identify it when it starts happening again. Because it will, and next time, we choose to move more quickly toward acceptance.

We focus our awareness in order to bring us all back into our present—not focusing on the future—and to bring back our control.

Third, when we have acceptance and awareness, we turn to *gratitude*. We tap into immense gratitude for the business, for the team, for our clients. We are even grateful for the people who place additional demands on our time, having gratitude that they are on the journey with the team and me. That gratitude helps bring back the joy into our organization and the team. Instead of seeing the situation as a burden, we hold joy in that space, and that choice lifts us back into our calmness.

As I navigate the Clickety-Clack, I also need to walk my talk with our work in The Pillar Code. The first practical tool I use is meeting with our practitioners, connecting, and receiving a treatment to align me back into calmness, acceptance, and control. With awareness, my confidence, and gratitude, I am able to navigate a pivotal time.

What tools do you recommend for staying peaceful in a seemingly toxic world?

First, find acceptance. Settle your mind. This process also appeases the subconscious, a part of ourselves that keeps us down and small. It protects us but also doesn't always allow us to succeed.

An action we created to move into acceptance of what is happening is to write what we call a *Fix-It-List*. We do this ourselves, and we ask our clients to do it as well. This list is not a task list, not a job list, but a fix-it list. We ask: *What in your life, in your business, in your world requires fixing?* As you write this list, consider all areas of your life. Once you create that Fix-It-List, it settles your mind and tells your subconscious you are doing something about it.

Then move into awareness of your *why*: Why is it important to take control of that journey? What is happening when you are not in control? Why are you not delivering your *why*? By returning to your *why*, your body of work comes together and lifts your consciousness into what you are doing.

Third, cultivate gratitude to experience the consistent faith of creating. Gratitude helps you respect all, manifest, and visualize. Every single day, our team remembers our future. We visualize it and then remember it. That practice will bring your soul into the process so the highest consciousnesses may come together.

These three tools are what we do to anchor our *why* and create our future. We remember our *why* in our goals and our manifestations and our visualizations. This connects us back to the first three pillars of The Pillar Code—Peace, Love, and Connection.

When we use these tools, everything comes into line, and we are off and running again—in peace. Love yourself, love your life, and stay connected. We are all about consciously connected leaders. This is a process that leads us to stay consciously connected.

About the Author

PJ is a Universal channel, business intuitive, mentor, and healer. In 2012, PJ received Universal information that we are currently at a turning point in humanity as truths are being revealed around the globe—generating great stress, anxiety, and illness.

PJ subsequently left a successful career in the corporate world to receive, develop, deliver, and teach the healing system: *The Pillar Code 12 Step Journey of Healing,* recognized in thirty-nine countries as a healing modality through the International Institute for Complementary Therapists.

The Pillar Code transforms clients from around the world as they connect to their highest potential and consciousness in all areas—life, mind, body, and business. As Founder and CEO, PJ and her team created an online university and practitioner training programs, and they released research of one hundred case studies revealing miraculous results. They also created a private membership group, The Creators Club.

PJ is a #1 bestselling author of *It's About Time by GEORGE*, detailing her amazing journey receiving Universal messages, and *Fast Forward to Success*, which she co-authored.

PJ is based near Canberra, Australia, and can be contacted at info@thepillarcode.com or thepillarcode.com. To register for The Creators Club, go to thepillarcode.com/the-creators-club. Use the promo code TCClubPJBOOK and receive your first month free or receive a year for the price of only nine months.

Claire Chitty

How has the Clickety-Clack shown up in your life?

For me, the Clickety-Clack has been the breath between challenging moments and experiences that allows momentous growth and positive change. Life has brought many lessons—both confronting and fulfilling—for spiritual expansion and a remembering of the divinity within. Reflecting on the past, I use the metaphor, *Life is like a tapestry*: one side of the material may appear in disarray, but on the other side, a colorful image starts to appear, formed from experiences, understanding, and knowledge.

My philosophy is to find the gift in each lesson, create wonderful memories, and make a positive difference in the world—whether offering a smile or a kind word or through my writing.

How did you navigate the Clickety-Clack?

Overcoming fear and mastering emotions has been a huge lesson for me, particularly during times of uncertainty and insecurity. I've chosen to experience a number of intense journeys in this life: anorexia, bulimia, sexual harassment, domestic violence, and workplace bullying. Eventually, these painful times have led to an awakening and deeper spiritual connection with myself and with Spirit.

Equally imperative is understanding, communication, and language. Words hold great power and can heal or harm. I avoid using *hard* and *difficult* and replace these words with *learning* and *challenging*. From personal experience, I have learned to avoid the phrases *I'm bored*, or *I want more excitement*.

The Universe doesn't differentiate between *good* and *bad*. Rather it works on vibration, frequency, and the resonance field. My language and thoughts brought some very uncomfortable lessons! Hence, through these confronting events, I learned the importance of being mindful and living moment to moment.

If life were a song, mine would be: *When the going gets tough, the tough get going*. A six-year journey within family law court to extract myself from a narcissist was an appalling nightmare. Every day was a challenge to endure, never knowing what tactic the ex-husband would play in a desperate attempt to discredit me. Anxiety was a byproduct of domestic violence and the court system, as I felt unsupported and helpless to change the situation.

Somehow, an inner strength and trust in a higher power kept me going through the tough days, despite being battle weary. The ongoing threats of violence behind closed doors taught me to differentiate between manipulation and coercion and to stand up for what was right for myself and my children. Despite all the games, forgiveness and journaling were practices I implemented, determined not to become bitter or manifest dis-ease in my body.

Apparently, my court case helped change a broken system for the better so that resources and support are more readily available for women.

What tools do you recommend for staying peaceful in a seemingly toxic world?

My two main tools for staying peaceful are *connecting to the heart*, and *connecting to the breath*. Without these two aspects, people often become destabilized and, therefore, feelings of overwhelm, anxiety, and imbalance may occur.

Cultivate the mind/body/soul connection to stay in a state of equilibrium by developing a daily spiritual routine: yoga, meditation, sound, a walk, being heart-centered, or something that resonates with you.

Daily, take time to meditate. Focus on the heart area, slow down the breath, and meditate with a mantra or a mandala or by simply observing the breath.

With commitment, intention, and practice, meditation creates a more peaceful existence. Life begins to flow with beautiful synchronicities, love, and joy. Thoughts become clearer. Although tests and challenges will still exist, they will have less impact. Mindfulness becomes a new way of living.

I include many tools on my list:

The Violet Flame is a favorite practice where any challenges are thrown into the flame to transmute, transform, and transcend ego and lower attachments.

Specific affirmations done with loving intention can be powerful as they restructure and rewire the brain. Handwrite affirmations and place them around predominate areas, including the bathroom mirror, your desk, and the fridge, as a friendly reminder to repeat throughout the day and maintain momentum. My favorite is: *All is well and I am safe.*

Crystals, crystal singing bowls, essential oils, homeopathic vials, Aura Soma color healing, and tapping are other tools I incorporate into my life and into client sessions. When combined with intention and love—the highest vibration—miracles occur.

Gratitude is powerful. The Universe loves a grateful heart. Avoid complaining—remember words are powerful and hold an energetic vibration.

My go-to quick recharge is a *brisk walk*, yet *connecting to the ocean, nature, or a hot springs spa* refreshes my soul more profoundly.

Writing, drawing, and spending time with family, great friends, and amazing mentors are other activities that fill my inner being.

Using my sensitivity, I can see, feel, and sense other people's energy. *Protecting my auric field* is a no-brainer, whether using a shield of light, the Armor of God, Archangel Michael, or another means.

Occasionally, *putting distance between me and a challenging individual* allows us both space and time to process whatever they are going through. There are several ceremonies; the easiest one is visualizing a large pink rose quartz between that person and me. This generally shifts, absorbs, and stabilizes the disharmony, allowing healing and transformation to occur.

With every challenge that presents itself, I go within and *ask what the underlying lesson is.* This practice provides a good time to heal and release old stories, beliefs, and conditioning. For me, doing *inner child and mirror work* is immensely valuable. In the past, it has brought up unhealed layers I thought I'd dealt with, along with copious amounts of tears. I'm happy to say that clearing issues, learning to say *no*, creating boundaries, and taking personal responsibility have made room for magic to manifest.

One final reflection: Always keep learning, growing, and evolving. We are all interconnected on this planet, and everything is energy. Therefore, as we individually work on ourselves, we automatically shift the collective consciousness in positive, powerful ways.

Are you ready to create a life of possibilities and potential?

About the Author

Claire Chitty was born clairaudient—along with the other clairs—and fully implemented these gifts in her twenties when Merlin, Archangel Michael, and angels appeared. Since then, many guides have materialized to her, including a Pleiadian mentor.

With over twenty-five years of experience in a variety of healing modalities, metaphysical kinesiology, health and nutrition, emotional freedom technique, and multidimensional healing that she describes as *Reiki on steroids*, Claire incorporates color, sound, and crystals into her wellness practice. Elemental space clearing and clutter clearing are also part of her diverse business.

Claire works with children, teens, and adults, both individually and in group sacred circles and meditation classes, to reactivate their bodies' healing energy systems.

She is also a passionate traveler, early childhood educator, and writer, specializing in children's picture and chapter books. Her first novel on teen mental health, *Love You, Love Me* (Austin

Macauley Publishers); and a junior fiction book, *Thoughts Out of My Head* (Leon Smith Publishing), about incorporating blended families, are due for release shortly.

If you're feeling fatigued, stressed, or destabilized, make the commitment and invest in your health and healing. To find out more, book a free twenty-minute consultation via Zoom. Or sign up with your email address to receive monthly discounts.

Contact Claire at: possibilitiesandpotential.com.au or email her at: possibilitiesandpotential@gmail.com.

Lottie Cooper

How has the Clickety-Clack shown up in your life?

The Clickety-Clack has shown up in my life recently. I was living in this beautiful bird sanctuary home with my sweetheart, and the owners decided they did not want to do a long-term rental anymore. They asked us to leave. I was in love with this place—it had bears and butterflies and dragonflies—and they gave us two weeks to find a new home.

On top of that, my mom called me and said she required brain surgery and needed me to come take care of her. We found a place to live within a few days, then before we unpacked, I had to jump on a plane. I was about to go to the airport when I received a text from the airline that all flights were canceled.

I thought to myself: *What do I do?*

I called the airlines and looked at different airports. There was a flight taking off that day from an airport two hours away. My sweetheart agreed to drive me the extra two hours to the airport. I got to the airport, jumped on the plane, and landed in Dallas. In Dallas, I boarded my second flight, but the plane was waiting on the airstrip. Waiting and waiting.

At midnight, we learned the pilot was overworked, so we couldn't take off. Then, the airline canceled the flight and claimed it was *due to weather.* There was no other flight. Next, we passengers found out they would not put us up in a hotel if a flight was changed because of *weather.* Many people chose to sleep on the chairs or on the ground in the airport or just stay up until morning. I wanted a good night's sleep to be present for my mother.

I hadn't unpacked anything in my new house. It was unfurnished. Then, I found myself stuck with no hotel—no nothing—standing in a long line. I finally found a hotel that wasn't full at three o'clock in the morning.

On very little sleep, I got up early, did my Kunlun meditation practice, and received a message from within to get a taxi and go to the airport. A woman in the lobby let me jump in her Uber to the airport. The flight departures screen on my phone said a flight was leaving in forty-five minutes, but I didn't know which gate. I went to customer service, but there was a long line.

Right next to me was a guy from American Airlines. I asked him for help, but he said, "I am stuck too."

I asked him, "Do you possibly know which gate I need to go to be on standby?"

He told me where the gate was, and I ran across the airport. I was able to get a flight that day, instead of waiting another day.

That is one example of the Clickety-Clack that I dealt with just this week.

How did you navigate the Clickety-Clack?

I have navigated the Clickety-Clack by communicating with God/Source. I have done it through grounding and clearing energy out of my body.

For example, I clear everyone else's fear out through a grounding process, using my aura and working with colors. I stay centered and connected to deep listening, which allows for synchronicity. From that place, I slow down and ask the right questions and let my inner guidance direct me. This practice is very useful.

I have worked with a variety of tools I also teach my clients, including self-acupressure to release tension, pain, headaches and heartache; inner-child wound work; family constellations; and theta healing. I stand in different energy fields, trying future possibilities. By feeling all the emotions, I can know ahead of time if a place is the right destination.

I also set my intention every day to be of greater service; this practice aligns me with the Universe.

Additionally, I have found it works to have an attitude of gratitude and to have deep compassion for everyone and anyone involved. When I have compassion for people, even strangers are helpful and loving. From that compassion, a lot of synchronicities show up—like the free ride to the airport, or meeting the airline person who told me where to go to catch that last flight, or when my boyfriend was willing to drive me an extra two hours to an airport.

When I am centered and aligned with right action, miracles show up around me, and I am attuned with the flow of life.

What tools do you recommend for staying peaceful in a seemingly toxic world?

First, *love and trust*. Be honest with yourself, and know that the Universe—or the multiverse—is abundant and full of love and light. Come from that framework and have compassion for whatever happens. I have learned to use my aura and colors, as I mentioned before. You can visualize your aura, the color around you. Choose the color you desire, and if you find anything unlike that color, you can send it instantly into the earth to transmute it into love and light. This technique is great for empaths. It's a reminder that you don't have to absorb everyone else's energy when you want to be connected with your own answers.

Next, *have an attitude of gratitude*; recognize that everyone is doing their best. Communicate from your heart honestly, even if you are not sure what other people are going to think. If they think negatively about you, just send that energy down the grounding cord and do not take it personally.

Also, *repattern your subconscious mind* to release negative beliefs, such as changing *I am not good enough* to *I am enough*. In my own mind, I have repatterned thousands of negative beliefs into positive ones, and I have helped thousands of people do the same, completely changing their lives. When you shift your inner critic into an inner mentor or cheerleader, life becomes abundantly better. You then can see and experience the best in yourself and in other people, uplifting everyone.

These tools and others have helped me navigate the Clickety-Clack. I have also learned to work with angels, which has been helpful. I teach others how to work with angels as well.

I support people in communicating. I have developed a tool I call *Instant Mind-Shift* that uses colors to help people change their perspective by clearing negativity and their charge. This also allows people to look at situations from multiple perspectives. When you do that, you allow others to have different perspectives. Then, everyone is right from their perspective, and you can understand them—instead of making one person more important than the other. Remember, it's not about being right.

What matters is that everyone is heard and understood. From that place of love, new perspectives and higher levels of communication, intimacy, and love can abound. That's what works for me.

About the Author

For over twenty years, Lottie Cooper has helped entrepreneurs, leaders, women and men, couples, coaches, empaths, Starseeds, HSPs, and business owners have more energy; stop self-sabotaging; and heal blocks, trauma, and communications that were slowing down their progress and limiting their ability to make changes.

Lottie has helped thousands of people find the root cause of their chronic issues, uncover hidden blind spots and limiting beliefs, and resolve them permanently. She uses unique techniques learned while gaining her master's in Body-Centered Clinical Psychology from Santa Barbara Graduate Institute, which then became part of the Chicago School of Professional Psychology.

She completed the Berkeley Psychic Institute's year-long Clairvoyant Women's training program, Suzanne's inner child work from Archangel Michael, William B. Tanran Reiki, Advanced Theta Healing, and over fifty other modalities.

She travels and teaches around the world, as well as teaches remotely over Zoom and phone to create individualized and group healing, business, and coaching programs. She has been a speaker on international stages; in telesummits; and for VIP days, intensives, and retreats in person and virtually.

Schedule a no-cost breakthrough call to uncover blocks, so you can move forward in your next steps. Spaces are limited. Go to: inspirationalcounseling.com or Lottiecooper.com. For people outside the United States, the best contact is via WhatsApp, 1-720-938-9627.

Facebook: facebook.com/CoachLottieCooper

LinkedIn: linkedin.com/in/LottieCooper

Heather Davis

How has the Clickety-Clack shown up in your life?

Truth be told, the Clickety-Clack has been riding shotgun with me since the day I was born. It has derailed many things in my life, but I wouldn't be here to tell this story had it not been for those diversions.

I grew up on a tiny farm in the deep south under the roof of an abusive alcoholic. The abuse I suffered created a deficit in my upbringing as I grew in the chrysalis of adolescence. I ran away from home many times, which sometimes resulted in additional abusive situations, such as rape and my own alcohol abuse. Thoughts of suicide most certainly swirled in my mind throughout various stages in my life.

All I wanted to do was escape my life. Eventually, I moved to Chicago in my early twenties. There, absolutely everything was different. I began reinventing myself; however, no matter how many new storylines I created in my head, the weight of abuse, low self-esteem, and loss still lingered in my heart. Amid the pain, I knew there was a higher plan for me—I just couldn't see it yet.

I met a doctor and fell in love. He was a closet alcoholic, but the relationship worked, as I knew exactly how to navigate that minefield. However, one step in that field changed the course of my life forever—pregnancy. Swimming in the sea of shame and fear at the thought of raising a child under an alcoholic, I had an abortion. It was truly the lowest moment of my life.

Two weeks later, I left the doctor and started attending AA. Every day, I grew stronger and started to remember that I was a child of God. I could not fully navigate the Clickety-Clack just yet, but I was gaining hope that I could. Once again, I felt the incredibly strong sensation that there was a higher plan for me.

At age thirty-four, I fell in love; married; and moved to North Carolina away from the hustle, bustle, and car horns. We created three beautiful miracle babies together, but not without the Clickety-Clack. We endured a traumatic birth with our first one that almost cost both our lives. By God's grace we both fully recovered, but I faced three years of PTSD therapy to heal.

There was a miscarriage along the journey, but in my heart someone was still missing from the table, so I persisted. One morning before school, my seven-year-old daughter was brushing her teeth when she suddenly stopped mid-action and looked up at me with a glaze over her eyes.

Foamy mouth and all, she stated, "I have a baby brother now."

I was in complete shock, yet a peaceful knowing came over me. At age forty-one, with complete joy in my heart, our baby boy came into the world. This third child brought the very breath of God upon me. Due to the damaging effects from the prior abortion and two births, he was never supposed to be, yet there he was—growing happily in my tummy. During this pregnancy, I felt, heard, and saw each moment through a heavenly lens.

My heavenly awakening had started. It was like being awakened from a great slumber. I could finally wipe the sand from my eyes and see my truth, my worth, and my capacity at the level God saw me. I questioned absolutely everything in my life. During this time, a higher plan was brought forth to me—one that I never saw coming.

I experienced visions. I was directed to open a plant-based wellness café, to help people heal from the inside out. I saw how my marriage was crumbling and there was no way for me to save it. I saw myself working with people in myriad ways to help heal their bodies, minds, and hearts. I was being called to great service, to leave behind what no longer served, and to allow God to rebuild me as He saw fit. I saw myself writing books, speaking to crowds, using God's healing energy, and—more than anything—spreading hope.

I wrote out a business plan for the café from a template I found on Google. I had never opened or owned a business before and had to learn everything from scratch. With the help of a friend and investor, I was able to bring to life the vision given to me. It was so much fun—and work—designing and branding the new concept that was different from anything else in this region. Under divine guidance, I wrote the entire menu myself.

In about a year's time, while still working my full-time day job, I opened the café. It was glorious, and our little community loved it. Then COVID hit. Yeah, that was a tough year. During 2020, I lost my sales career, my café, my marriage, and my home. I call it *The Great Shift* era. With hardly any savings, I applied for food stamps, rental assistance, and Medicaid at age forty-five, for the first time in my life. Under the seemingly unending cloud of divorce and loss, the kids and I ate off borrowed plates and slept on borrowed beds for an entire year.

However, this time the weight of my hurt and loss had a place to rest. It wasn't easy, but I knew how to take my suffering to God and allow Him to transform my mess into a miracle and my trial into a triumph. I could now see where He had transformed me time and time again throughout my life journey. Where once I could see only loss and misfortune, I now saw the lotus flower rising to bloom from the mud and muck. This perspective allowed the The Great Shift to take place.

I was called back into the chrysalis once more, this time growing within the radical faith that would foster both my highest good and all the gifts I had been born with in this lifetime. My foundation was rebuilt over that year. I spent hours in prayer and gratitude for not only my daily needs being met, but for the way forward to be shown to me. I walked with my head held high, firm in the promise that my best life was yet to come. Hope ran through my veins the way water is absorbed into thirsty ground.

How did you navigate the Clickety-Clack?

I first had to stop running from my past—and present—and work to lovingly embrace my story. AA was my kickstarter, and I still work on my codependency, PTSD, and abuse recovery daily through devotionals and meditation. The daily meditation practice changed my life. There was a lot of surrender that took place on my bathroom floor in tears of exhaustion, as I was a stubborn one. Ha!

I learned how to be present in my body, as it has been my chariot through so many journeys. No matter how I felt about it or what

I asked it to carry, which was a lot, my body continues to serve me, and I needed to honor that.

Mother Nature has been my teacher in much of this learning ever since I was a child, so I turned to her once again. My next steps seemed clearer after a hike or a walk in the woods.

I learned how to be present with the emotions in my body and to listen to the intelligence of those emotions. Emotions of fear, shame, grief, anger, hurt, mistrust, and even joy all had countless stories to tell of why they were there, how they came to be, and their longing to be released and freed.

I learned I was safe to feel within my body, that I was protected, and that healing truly was available to me, no matter what I had done in my past. The hope I felt was a real and tangible directive for me to keep moving forward.

In this surrendered learning, I finally accepted that I could not win the battles set before me alone; in fact, I was never supposed to fight them alone. I accepted that I have an entire army of angels assigned to walk this life and carry the sword for me, so the highest path ahead is always illuminated. Learning how to be present helped me see that path; mediation helped me learn how to be present in the journey.

The *messes* are there to get our attention, to unearth things that are ready to be healed, and always to work for us, not against us. It's in The Great Shift of perspective that we step into our own sovereignty, truth, and self-love—to see the miracle within the mess and faithfully expect the triumph from the trial.

What tools do you recommend for staying peaceful in a seemingly toxic world?

If we pause to ask our bodies and emotions a few questions, we can usually derive the best way forward. Sometimes, that way forward requires uncomfortable action or change that may be hard to accept, but acknowledging its presence is the first step.

In my healing practice for my clients, my audience, or myself, I often facilitate the below approach with great success. I like to call it the *Rainbow Experience* because it can bring freedom, hope, and joy back into their lives when other modalities have failed.

Step 1   Pause and take a few deep breaths to center your mind and take your thoughts into your heart space. The heart is where all good things live. While in the heart space, access the location in your body in which you are holding the emotion you are feeling. You'll be surprised that it's not always in the heart space.

Step 2:   Allow your love light to take you to the place in your body holding your emotion. Gently, speak words of love to the emotion, letting it know you want only to help, and you are here to listen. Introduce yourself with your birth name to this emotion and its energy. Think of this emotion as a small, helpless child in search of nourishment. To heal something, it must be tended to with great care. You can even give the emotion a name, like Tony, or a funny, made-up name like Ziggydoo. Maybe the emotion has a name it wants to give you. Be open to hearing this.

Step 3:   Ask exactly what emotion it is and try to pinpoint its nature (e.g., fear, grief). Ask: *Why are you here? What are you trying to show me or communicate to me? Is this emotion even mine, or did I by chance pick up someone else's emotion while speaking with them or spending time with them?*

Step 4:   After listening and feeling the needs of this emotion, encourage it to allow you to free it. You have taken note of its request and urgency. If needed, you can revisit that notation and plan to further heal the need shown to you. Our God created us to live in joy and bliss. Ask this emotion to trust you in leading it back into a joyful and blissful state. Note that most emotions belonging to you will revisit you if you do not act on the healing, whether it's an emotional or physical release needing to occur. Sometimes, the two can be intertwined. Allow your heart to guide you through, one step at a time.

Step 5:   Thank the emotion for coming to you, whether it has been as a protective presence, as a trauma that has plagued you over the years, or as a calling to release what no longer serves you and holds you back.

Step 6:   Release it! Allow it to bubble up and float away from your body. Ask Mother Nature to absorb this energy and transform it into love.

About the Author

Heather is an author, inspirational speaker, medical intuitive, Reiki master, and sound healer.

Five years ago, Heather's journey led her to open a spiritual coaching practice called The Lotus Soul, LLC. As a coalescent energy medicine practitioner, Heather uses sound, meditation, Earth elements, healing touch, intuitive mediumship, and Divine guidance in her healing facilitation.

In 2022, Heather started a speaking ministry, called *Light for the Path*, to help teach people how to find peace, understanding, and unseen miracles during the hardships in life. Her speeches focus on the experiences she has lived through, how she found freedom, and the radical miracles that followed. Her highest hope is that by sharing her voice, others will be encouraged in their healing and share their own.

She is the author of *Radiate Your Light*, a plant-based cookbook that incorporates easy, nourishing recipes that correspond with the body's chakra system. She is currently working on her spiritual memoir, *Rise*, a story about moving from fear to faith, against all odds.

Heather lives in North Carolina with her two miracle kiddos and their furry sidekick. When she's not speaking and writing, she can be found in the garden or hiking in the Carolina mountains.

To learn more about Heather and her services or simply to catch some good vibes, visit: Instagram @The.Lotus.Soul, Facebook @TheLotusSoul, or TheLotusSoul.com.

Sally Estlin

How has the Clickety-Clack shown up in your life?

When I was in my twenties, I was working in banking and finance, and it just did not feel right. It was good money, but it was quite a toxic environment. This is ultimately what led me to study natural therapies and alternative medicine.

When I was married and had four kids, I didn't feel aligned with myself and my life. I could not sleep at night. I was finding my soul, and I did not really understand what was going on. The environment we were living in did not sit right with me, so I left the marriage, which was a hard decision since four kids were involved.

Trying to navigate that time was tricky because I was trying to survive while experiencing a spiritual awakening. I was traveling down a spiritual path, starting to understand and discover my true self. I was experiencing greater awareness and consciously waking up, but my family and others surrounding me were not.

I always felt I was on the spiritual path, and my kids and loved ones were on a more superficial one because we were living in what felt like a toxic environment. I was healing my broken heart and finding the ways to do it, trying to exist in a very superficial world, all while I was on this spiritual path. It felt as if my soul was being crushed.

After years of looking after the kids, driving them everywhere, and leading a full life, everything changed when COVID hit. It was pretty challenging at the time, particularly because I was living in Melbourne, Australia. My kids were not living with me through the pandemic, and I went from a life of *everything* to having nothing. I felt isolated.

That was certainly a time when the Clickety-Clack showed up. Nothing felt aligned, and nothing was flowing. I did not feel grounded. I felt scattered and lost. So, the journey has been an ongoing process. It started in my twenties when I felt out of alignment and then left the marriage in my forties. I remodeled myself and my life to find the secret to life and what I really wanted. I am now in my fifties.

Not feeling right inside has probably been my biggest challenge—getting out of my head and into my heart and into my gut—thinking: *This alignment is not working for me. This world I live in is not working for me.* I needed to learn what I was supposed to be doing.

How did you navigate the Clickety-Clack?

I totally immersed myself in self-development and personal growth. I did healing work, and I started consciously connecting with myself. The turning point for me happened one day as I was walking down the stairs—this is when I was still married—going into the kids' rumpus room to turn the TV off. Oprah happened to be on television, and it was her final show. She did not have all the gifts and giveaways; she was alone on the stage for probably the last five minutes of her show. She said, "If there is one thing that I would pass on to everybody, it is to trust the niggle inside, the little voice in your head, that thing you feel does not make sense."

I have followed her advice since that day. That was a turning point for me because I started to say: *Hey, yes! I have been getting that niggle, those voices. I have been telling them to shut up for ages.* That was about thirteen years ago, and I have been following that path ever since.

I follow the energy. It does not make sense half the time, but it has always taken me down the right path. I just trust my gut. Trusting and believing are two key things I do and have done since I heard Oprah's words: trust my inner voice, trust the process, trust in myself, and believe that it will be okay. I am like a sponge; I am always learning, growing. I am reading so many supportive books that help me understand myself—help me grow and learn.

Walking in nature is my thing. I go out every day and walk out in nature. It has been back to basics, particularly since COVID. I love getting out in nature, walking, being grounded, breathing, and doing walking meditations; these are fantastic ways of connecting in with myself and processing life. I need time and space to allow that process to happen, and walking in nature gives that to me.

Also, working out is a huge element of my life. I work out with a girlfriend, and we process things. We talk about everything. Our talks are cathartic and healing, and they help me learn, grow, and stay balanced to deal with the stuff around me every day, the normality of life.

Meditation also is important to me, and doing Joe Dispenza's work took me to another level. Attending his advanced retreat helped me connect and move into the Quantum space. I do a lot of healing work, particularly in the dimensional realm, or the Quantum realm. That's a way you can allow yourself to just *be*.

I have done a lot of transformation work with my business, from running a physical gym that morphed into a metaphysical business to running workshops to help others and myself find our inner connection. When I work with my clients, I am healing myself as I facilitate their healing.

Living in the moment is one way I get through life, realizing I cannot change anything that happened in the past. Anything in the future is just a negative projection of stuff that has not even happened yet, which leads to worry and stress. I try to be in the now moment as much as possible. In the space of the present moment, I can truly create the life of my dreams—manifest to my full potential.

Another thing I do that helps me thrive is surround myself with like-minded people. I like to say that English is my second language. The language I use with consciously connected people is my first language.

I sit with gratitude and positivity every day. I have rituals in the morning, a gratitude ritual and calling in the Universe to assist with what I would like to draw in that day. These rituals help me stay in the driver's seat of my thoughts, my feelings, and my actions.

What tools do you recommend for staying peaceful in a seemingly toxic world?

Breathing is so important. Breathing helps us connect and flow effortlessly. Having awareness of yourself is key because you cannot change what you do not know. So allow yourself to breathe and be in the moment.

I also have a mantra that I work with myself and my clients: *Let go, Step up, and Be more of you.* Be more of you in the present moment. We do not need to *do* more, we just need to *be* more. Be more in the moment, be your authentic self. Be more, and then you can be a beacon of life and radiate or echo love and light. People are so attracted to love and light as they resonate. People are drawn to this beautiful energy as it goes out. Just be the beacon of light in the present moment.

Sit with positivity and gratitude because every situation can be perceived positively or negatively. It's your choice. I choose to stay in a positive light; everything can be turned around as it shifts with positive energy. So, be in the moment and do everything from this stabilized space.

Be more of yourself and do more of what you love and what brings you happiness. That is what is sacred; it's most important. Do more of what you love, and it will make you happy. For me, it's being out in nature and working out. I highly encourage you to go out into nature to walk and ground—and be near water. It's very cathartic. I work out because I feel good; you can do it with like-minded girlfriends or friends.

Empower each other and workshop through stuff together. Surround yourself with positive people, positive like-minded people who speak the same language as you. It is so comforting, and you won't feel weird, as nothing is woo-woo. You can speak on a deeper, connected level. Whatever personal growth and healing you do will make you more comfortable in your skin; you will be more able to enjoy yourself, to be at peace.

Be a sponge. Listen, learn, and act. Listen to as much inspiring or educational material as you can. Listen to your body, as it has something to say. Learn from it and act. Action is important because words are cheap with no actions behind them. Being like a sponge will help you upscale, gaining deeper personal growth.

Trust and believe in yourself. Let go of people's judgments and opinions. Stay comfortable in your own skin and trust yourself. Trust the process. Believe in yourself.

Manifest like crazy. The key to manifesting is feeling as if you have it, right here, right now, but you must practice when you are in the now, stabilized in the present moment. It is such a beautiful feeling. Then amplify it with gratitude and clarity.

Heal those wounds. You can never stop evolving. Life is too short to feel crappy when we can have a happy life. You know, I am all about going from good to great, from average to awesome. Connect with yourself and keep growing. Heal your wounds. Create the life of your dreams. It is all about being more of you and staying anchored in the present moment.

To stay peaceful in a seemingly toxic world, follow your mantra and let go of stuff that does not matter, that really does not count. Step up and be more of yourself, more of you in the moment. Allow yourself to radiate out as a beacon of love and light.

About the Author

Sally Estlin is a Holistically Fit specialist based in Melbourne, Australia. Her passion is helping people *Let Go, Step Up, and Be More* of themselves, to live a more aligned and purposeful life. She helps people break through their barriers to create positive change.

Sally founded Holistically Fit by following her love for health, fitness, and general well-being. It started as a personal training business and evolved to focus on deeper personal growth and energy healing. Based on her experience and in-depth learnings, particularly with natural therapies and alternative medicine, her interest is working with the *whole* individual, integrating the mind, body, and soul.

Sally incorporates a myriad of tools and techniques. Her services range from personal training to hands-on healing, online coaching, and remote energy work.

Sally has published a *30-day Wellness Mindset Journal*, offers intuitive card readings, and is a Wellness Coach, quantum healer and activator, change agent, personal trainer, podcaster, and co-host on an international networking group HNP. She hosts the *Your Holistically Fit Life* show on the Natural TV Channel on Roku TV and is currently working on a self-empowerment fashion label.

Sally is guided by her intuition and follows the energy in all areas of life. She has four incredible kids and loves being in nature, exercising, and workshopping life. Sally is passionate about helping people heal and grow quickly and deeply.

Visit her website, holisticallyfit.com.au, or
email: sally@holisticallyfit.com.au.

Are you a worrier or a warrior? Take the test and find out here: holisticallyfit.com.au/warriortest.

Order your Wellness Mindset Journal:
holisticallyfit.com.au/journal.

Let's have a chat! holisticallyfit.com.au/book-a-call/.

Nadine Felix

How has the Clickety-Clack shown up in your life?

Resilience. How many times have I heard or used this trendy word without it truly resonating? Up until these last five years, resilience was simply a concept to me. A beautiful idea.

Today, I can honestly say to you: *Resilience is felt; it is lived.* But for this to be true, you have to see your whole life turned upside down. You have to go through hell and find yourself at the bottom of the water. There, you have only two choices left—let yourself slowly slide further, attracted by the intoxicating depth, or give a good kick to the bottom and rise to the surface.

I made my choice. I made my choice when the crucial moment arrived, when I thought I'd been through it all, known it all, suffered it all, and cried all I could.

I was a journalist, a good journalist on TV and radio. Then I was quickly made manager and then station director for TV and radio for the largest audiovisual group in France.

My work took me all over the world. First in French Guiana— my home country, a French territory in South America—where I began my career. I was later transferred to French Polynesia, where I spent three years, and then on to the small pebble of

Saint-Pierre and Miquelon where I spent eighteen months. What a shock the cold was over there!

It was during these many years of exile, alongside my husband and youngest son, I saw my life turned upside down. Over a short period of time, my father, one of my sisters, and then my mother passed away. It was a real tragedy—an explosion in our country where our family was far from anonymous. My parents were well-known musicians and both teachers of their craft.

And my sister, my little sister! I still have a hard time believing it. We didn't see it coming. We couldn't have. At forty-four years old, illness stole her away from us in just two months.

This was a time of terrible mourning—a shock for my poor mother. She put on a brave face, but a ruptured aneurysm stole her away just a few months later. Three bereavements, one after the other. Awful!

But despite it all, my brother, my two sisters, and I made it through with dignity.

My main sanctuary during this time became my job. However, deep inside me, I nourished the secret hope of returning home. Finally, I expressed it.

But no.

It was then, during this same year, I was sent to Guadeloupe to be responsible for a company of 200 people. Except this time, on top of the exile and all the grief I was working my way through, I also came face to face with loneliness. Tired and emotionally exhausted, my husband and my youngest son, then seventeen years old, did not follow me to Guadeloupe. Instead, they returned together to French Guiana.

I was by myself when I landed on this French Caribbean island.

At almost the exact same time as my arrival, COVID-19 came. We had to manage, organize, and continue sharing information while protecting everybody from the virus. We did it. While the unions have a reputation for being especially tough there, and other companies suffered protests and strikes, they played ball with us and proved themselves true partners.

I'm a worker—a hard worker. I became totally involved, so much so that I forgot myself. All of a sudden, stress became a part of my daily life, until it took over, despite all the warnings my doctor gave me.

Yet, even with all these complications, I saw only green lights ahead, and I continued to receive excellent ratings at my work. Especially as I believe in management through kindness. Putting people at the heart of the project, listening to employees, and not treating them like numbers were particularly important to me. And you know what? Management through kindness works. I applied it, and it works.

Perhaps it worked too well in the eyes of some. My methods were certainly a step away from the usual way of doing things—not to mention that my name started circulating in the group. I was stopped in mid-swing. Overnight, after only fourteen months on the island, I found myself at a crossroads: I had the choice to either passively accept what others had decided for me—

Or not.

I was not prepared for it. I never even imagined this rare moment of violence, of nameless brutality could happen. I looked adversity straight in the eye.

I was simply dumped. Without notice. They instructed me to return to Paris to sit on the shelf.

Yet on this day, at this precise moment, I said no. No. NO.

How did you navigate the Clickety-Clack?

This day put an end to my twenty-five-year-long career and my settled life.

It put me on the edge of the precipice while I was making a good living.

It confronted me with the unknown future of which I knew nothing.

In a fraction of a second, I was hit hard by the five wounds: rejection, abandonment, humiliation, betrayal, and injustice.

I felt the rug being pulled out from under my feet. Everything I had worked so hard for was being taken away from me, just like that.

I should have panicked. I could have begged. I should have cried, threatened to sue (as everyone suggested I do), or fought for myself.

But I smiled. I just smiled. And I said *no*.

It was like an out-of-body experience. I was watching myself, so calm, so serene. I heard myself refuse, realizing at the same time all that my words implied. Saying no was choosing to quit my job, to quit this group—to find myself without employment from one day to the next, all at the height of my career. It was also facing the gaze of others, a humiliation.

It was a real turning point in my life, but deep down, I was at peace. At that precise moment, my soul took over, and for the very first time, I let it happen. My inner self spoke, and for once, I listened.

Without the slightest anguish—at least not at that time—and without any worry for what was to follow, I was simply liberated and experienced supreme relief. By saying no to my boss, I regained control of the situation, I regained control of my life, and at the same time, I withdrew from the role of the victim.

Maybe one of the worst days of my life.

Definitely one of the most liberating days of my life.

The day I learned to surrender to life, to trust life, to trust my faith, to trust myself.

The day I was able to say: *resilience, here I am!*

What tools do you recommend for staying peaceful in a seemingly toxic world?

The essence of the message that I want to convey is that there is nothing, no test in the world, from which we cannot recover. Once we have integrated it, we reduce the fear.

I have often been told throughout my life: *You are such a strong woman.*

Maybe.

What I know, above all, is that I am not alone. I am helped. I am constantly guided. We all are. We can give it the name that speaks to us best, but God, the Universe, the Source, the divine

Energy, the Force of life never leaves us. When we have intimate faith in it, then we are strong.

But do we even know how to hear it?

It is nonetheless there, this light. It is there, deep within us. This divine part in us is just waiting for the moment to free itself to let us shine completely. When we let it express itself, then, and only then, do we feel that we are there. Serenity sets in because doubt is not allowed. We know: *This is it!*

How many times a day do we act a certain way when everything inside of us is crying out for us to take another direction?

How many times a day do we do things contrary to our own desires? How many times in a lifetime do we stubbornly go in a direction that doesn't suit us, makes us sick, and slowly shuts us down?

How many of us feel lost and no longer find meaning in our lives?

The signs are there. They are not always spectacular shows; they are sometimes just small signals that we swat away with the sweep of our hand. In crucial moments, we need to listen to ourselves more than ever.

Our inner guide speaks. Sometimes it even tries to take over. At the time of my transfer to Guadeloupe, everything in me told me not to go under those conditions. My husband and my son listened, but I did not.

I was called by duty. I was needed. My ego was flattered by this new job offer. But deep down inside, I only wanted one thing—to join my family in French Guiana.

Finally, it is essential that we do not give in to the role of being the victim.

I am not a victim.

I am not a victim.

I am not a victim.

Repeating this sentence mentally allows you to keep hold of the reins and not hand over power to our supposed executioner.

Take the reins. This is one of the most powerful secrets to not losing control.

> *I am the master of my fate:*
> *I am the captain of my soul.*
> ~ William Ernest Henley
> "Invictus"

To be completely honest, once this particular moment has passed, in the days that follow, you will be met with doubt, anguish, anger, grief, and a deep feeling of injustice along with the four other wounds previously mentioned. You need to be able to get through it, but above all, you need to know how to make it out.

It is here that I must thank my husband, my children, and all my relatives who have supported me enormously. I also give thanks to my country, which has always been there for me. And I can't forget my many friends. Thanks to all this support, I have not lost my way.

Moreover, I am an unconditional fan of Nelson Mandela, whom I particularly admire for his ability to forgive. For almost a year,

I filled entire notebooks in an attempt to forgive. I sent light and love to this unprecedented situation for me, to the people I could have blamed, and I gave thanks, thanks, and thanks again for this moment that allowed me to grow.

It was extremely difficult at first. But day after day, the energy I put into it allowed me to feel my heart calm down, and a tremendous hope opened up before me.

Since then, I have created a club, the Sorella Club, a sorority to support women, and in particular those who are in positions of responsibility and going through a difficult period.

I have also created a consulting and coaching business, and a third project is coming. My family has reunited, life is smiling at me like never before, and love reigns supreme over everything around me.

At fifty years old, I opened up a whole new chapter in my life. With my experience and gifts in public speaking, I want to spread my message around the world: If we listen to each other, if we believe in ourselves, if we trust in life, if we place love at the center of it all, nothing can stop us. Thank you, Life. Thank you, God. Thank you, Me.

And although it is not from my culture, I want to conclude with these inspiring words from Maya Angelou:

> I'm a woman
>
> Phenomenally.
>
> Phenomenal woman,
>
> That's me.

About the Author

Nadine Félix is from French Guiana, a French department located in the heart of the Amazon rainforest in South America. Born to passionate musicians, she is the eldest of five siblings.

Married and mother of two children, today Nadine is an author, speaker, and certified coach. She shares her resolutely positive vision of life and her love for others throughout the world.

Nadine's passion is journalism, in which she pursued a career beginning in 1996. She had a brilliant twenty-five-year career at France Télévisions as a journalist but also as a manager, editor-in-chief, and regional director. It was this job that led her far from home to French Polynesia, Saint-Pierre, Miquelon, and Guadeloupe.

In 2021, on the threshold of her fiftieth birthday, she opened a new chapter in her professional life. She founded the Sorella Club and bears witness to painful moments that turned her life upside down. Her message: No matter what challenges we encounter, we can overcome them. Through the Sorella Club, she works with women and brings inspiring figures to light through her thought-provoking interviews. She invites you to visit sorellaclub.com to learn how they can help you too.

Do not hesitate to get in touch with Nadine Félix, who will share openly with you her faith in life and the trust that animates and guides her: nadine.felix@sorellaclub.com.

Maureen Marhayla

How has the Clickety-Clack shown up in your life?

One way the Clickety-Clack showed up for me was in the form of anxiety and panic attacks. I experienced them in public, especially in crowds. My heart would race. I'd sweat, shake, lose my cool, and then shut down. Sometimes, there would even be tears and hysterical sobbing if I could find a place that felt safe enough for me to hide. These attacks started to limit where I would go and what I wanted to do. I felt trapped.

Now, this may not sound like it was a positive shifting of gears or upleveling in my life, but eventually, it did end up that way. All these feelings I had exiled deep in my body and unconscious were coming up as panic and anxiety to let me know I had places that needed healing. After a while, I became so uncomfortable that I had to do *something* to deal with it.

How did you navigate the Clickety-Clack?

I feel like I tried everything, approaching it from all perspectives—physical, mental, emotional, soul, and spiritual.

It all helped, but what had the biggest impact was the idea of creating *Heaven on Earth*. This foundation allowed me to be fully present with myself to heal. I was able to remember the truth of my essence, stand in my power, and offer my gifts and blessings to the world.

Creating Heaven on Earth

Trauma, wounding, anxiety, and overwhelm cause a severing of connection—from our own self; from the Earth; from the Divine; from our family, friends, and community. This technique of creating Heaven on Earth begins the process of *reconnection* that is a crucial part of healing. When what's happening outside and inside of me is too much for me to handle and my body freaks out into panic and overwhelm, creating Heaven on Earth helps me manage it. This space allows me to stay calm and present—to be able to process what's going on, with support.

When we are experiencing intense emotions, it is helpful to have some support to assist us in the process of being in the *here and now* with those emotions. Sometimes the feelings are too much for us to hold alone, so we can use a strong, energetic container to hold us, to hold our emotions, and to hold our reactions. Some people call this energetic container *Sacred Space, Power Space, Safe Space, Brave Space, or Supportive Space*. I call it Heaven on Earth. The purpose of this container is to anchor us in the here—our body, the Earth—and now—present moment—surrounded by the support of the Divine. This is the only true place of power.

Heaven on Earth is a space of connection and love. It is all around us, all the time. We access it just by acknowledging it.

To begin, I honor the Earth that holds me with love. All I really have to do is say out loud, or to myself: *Thank you, Earth for holding me, so sweetly, so abundantly.* To strengthen this connection, I sometimes place my hand on the ground or offer a gift to the Earth, such as a pinch of lavender buds I have blown a prayer of gratitude into or a splash of water I have prayed into.

Next, I call to the Great Spirit that flows through all things—by whatever name appeals to me—with gratitude for its presence. Sometimes I will include an acknowledgement of ancestors, angels, or any other Helping Spirits who love me. Again, I can say: *Great Spirit*—or Divine Mother, or Heavenly Father, or Energy of Life that infuses all things, or God, or Allah, or whatever language I want to use—*thank you for dancing with us to the song of life.* Sometimes I like to light a candle to represent the light of the Divine.

So we now have Heaven and Earth accounted for. The last step is for me to acknowledge myself as a bridge between the two great forces. I am affirming the presence of my Higher Self, the part of me that *knows* as it acts as a connector between Heaven and Earth. If I know I will be interacting with others, I will affirm the presence of their Higher Selves as well.

This practice allows me to trust that all involved will show up with more than just their personality or ego-self. I know we will be engaging one another from a place of love, honor, and respect. To do this, I may say: *I affirm my spirit and the spirit of* name of other people *as we connect for the highest good of all concerned.*

This process can be as simple as a thought, spoken prayer, or invocation. Or it can be more complex, involving ceremony, song, movement, art, or whatever you would like, to add to the foundational process I describe. You can use your own words to personalize this technique. It can be done alone or in a group. You can do it daily, or occasionally, as you choose.

When I affirm that I am living in Heaven on Earth, I am reminded that I am held by the love and support of the Universe, and this gives me the strength to face whatever shows up. I am able to be present for myself and others. I began doing this before going into crowds, before healing sessions, and whenever I started to feel overwhelmed, and soon I was feeling more peace. I was able to do the things I used to love and began to enjoy new things. This was a gift of freedom for me.

Blessing the World

Once we have created Heaven on Earth, it is up to us to decide what we want to do from this space. I was able to do so much healing for myself, and then I learned how to do healing work for my family too. Since my anxiety sprung from being around strangers, I never really intended to work with others. But you know that old saying, *Make a plan and watch God laugh.*

Eventually, circumstances drew me into working with other people as well. Together, we create Heaven on Earth. We are held and supported by the nurturing Earth, we are filled with the energy of the Divine, and we invite blessings of healing and wholeness to help people remember the truth of their essence. It is such a gift to hold space for others as they do their own beautiful, empowering work, and to see them then be able to offer their gifts out to bless the world. It is a beautiful cycle of receiving and giving.

I think of a blessing as an energetic transmission that comes from both the divine, heavenly realms, and the earthly realm. Often, it contains a little bit of the energy of the one offering the blessing, as well, and leads to healing and wholeness for the receiver. It clears away what no longer serves you and fills you up with light, grace, and support. It reconnects you to yourself so you can remember the truth of your essence—your beauty, wisdom, gifts, power, and destiny. It also reconnects you to Earth, Heaven, and others.

When we are able to stand in our power, connected to Heaven and Earth, and be truly present to ourselves and those around us, then we become the place of Heaven on Earth. Our presence becomes a blessing to the world. We are all capable of offering blessings whenever we choose. We can bless with our words, our actions, our eyes, our thoughts and prayers, our hands, our feet, our bodies, and our creations. There really are no limits to how we can shine our light and love out into the world.

I'd like to leave you with a blessing to help you navigate the moments of the Clickety-Clack in your life.

Clickety-Clack Blessing

When you find yourself in a seemingly toxic and shifting state,

> May you feel held by the Earth.

> May you be filled with the light of Heaven.

> May you be healed.

> May you be whole.

> May you remember your holiness and create Heaven on Earth.

> May you stand in your power and offer your gifts and blessings into the world.

May your journey through the Clickety-Clack bless you, and

May you use the blessings of this time to bless the world.

What tools do you recommend for staying peaceful in a seemingly toxic world?

Create Heaven on Earth as often as you would like. From this space, be present to yourself and others with love. Feel the peace of this connection with the Earth, the Divine, yourself, and others.

Do whatever healing work you feel called to do for yourself from the space of Heaven on Earth.

Bless yourself. Invite blessings into your life. Look for the blessings to show up. Be open to receive them. Express gratitude for your blessings.

Bless the World. Intend to bless others. You can bless people, places, animals, or things. Pay attention to what calls to your heart and bless that. Shine your love and light out into the world in ways that delight you.

About the Author

Maureen Marhayla is a healer, teacher, blessing giver, stone reader, ceremony leader, shamanic energy practitioner, mystic, and mother of four adults. She is a graduate of the Four Winds Healing the Light Body School, has studied with teachers of core shamanism, and has studied and sat in ceremonies with healers in Peru. She has a Ph.D. in Educational Psychology. She is also a student of Healing Touch. She loves trees, rocks, vibrant colors, reading, sitting by water, and Diet Pepsi with lime.

She'd love to connect further with you:

Facebook: Maureen Marhayla

Instagram: @maureen.marhayla

Website: maureenmarhayla.com

Register on her website to receive more information on "Tips for Coping with Feeling Overwhelmed."

Nami Nesterowicz

How has the Clickety-Clack shown up in your life?

The Clickety-Clack showed up in 2020: My wife had cancer, my teenage son was in crisis, and our metaphysical shop could have only ten clients inside at a time during COVID. The line of customers waiting to come in would sometimes wrap around the building, and they would get frustrated. Additionally, I could not go to the hospital with my wife. I could not go with her to chemo treatments. During the long hours she was in treatment, I would go to Whole Foods to find healthy meals for her to eat. She had a short window of opportunity after chemo when she could eat without being nauseous, so I felt a lot of time pressure, as well as grief and guilt that I couldn't be with her.

I saw my son only on Thursdays, so I would bring him to lunch to create bonding time. At our metaphysical shop, called *The Bag Lady—Intuitive Gifts*, I would make jokes with people to keep them entertained while waiting in line. The line formed behind our building, sometimes up to fifty people. I would talk with them and tell them it was okay. I explained that since churches and schools were not meeting in person, this was the time for healing within ourselves and being one with each other. Then, I would point out they could purchase the things they needed, such as Palo Santo, candles, and rocks for protection and for healing.

It was very trying; I did not realize I was in the Clickety-Clack at that time. It felt as if it was never going to end. Every day, I had to be the one constantly in the center, grounded in oneness, and showing up for people and myself—the presence of steadiness.

How did you navigate the Clickety-Clack?

Keeping true to myself and my responsibilities became a full-time occupation:

- I took classes with healer and author Cyndi Dale; I completed about fifty hours with her during this time.

- I meditated every day, at least two or three times a day.

- I went to acupuncture to help release what no longer served me and to help stay centered.

- I would visit the waterfall in our backyard to balance and stay balanced.

- I would paint.

- I would drum.

- I would do anything to keep energy flowing within so that I would not lose who I was in the midst of all the chaos.

Again, I had to stay in the presence of Oneness, of God, of the Universal Light, making sure that I was cared for as well. If I did not wear my mask, I could not help anybody else wear theirs.

Because, as they say before every journey on a plane, we must put on our oxygen masks first.

I was reminded of that every day—to keep my oxygen mask on so I could help other people.

What tools do you recommend for staying peaceful in a seemingly toxic world?

I use tree essences that I receive from Canada; these help me stay grounded and centered. They get to the root of the problem because the trees have deep roots. If you can reach the root of your issue, it will help you fulfill your destiny, help you get rid of things that no longer serve you.

Writing became important to me as well. I would journal my thoughts for the day, any complications that happened, and then my gratitudes. This shifted me out of fear. I journal still, and I recommend keeping a journal of your own.

I sought others to talk to. I am a talker, so if I say something three times, I am able to let it go. When I felt fear, I would count to ten and then list my gratitudes because it shifted my attitude.

A gentleman from Tibet came to our shop and sold us some Tibetan singing bowls. He told me their vibrations can help ground you and help you let things go as well. He taught me how to do sound baths by putting my feet in a large brass bowl while striking the sides of the bowl in the four directions. While you are *in* the bowl, place your intentions and the items you wish to release inside with you. Then the vibrations will help you move them out.

I would move my mallet in a circle on the gong to warm it up and then hit the center of it with the intention of bringing the kundalini through my chakras. I was able to release anxiety and fear through that practice.

I did a lot of inner child work, saying *Ho'oponopono*:

I love you.

I am sorry.

Please forgive me.

Thank you.

In gratitude.

In classes with Cyndi Dale, she taught us how to bring in the *superluminal realm* and the *subluminal realm*. The subluminal realm is below our foundation and rises up through us, so we can feel the ground. The superluminal realm is above the Universe, and it brings the universal codes, the universal Akashic records, so that we have the knowledge we need. We realize we are in the Oneness, grounded in the Oneness of the Universe. We can bring heaven on Earth through those realms.

About the Author

Nami Nesterowicz is a healer, channeler, angel painter, and author. He's been in the healing profession since 1995, offering guidance and mentoring for students of all ages. Nami helps clients hone their innate intuitive skills, developing them further and unlocking abilities they may not have discovered yet.

There are many ways to connect with Nami. He teaches about the archangels, from Michael to Gabriel to Milagros, and more. He teaches students how to experience their energies and then directs them to help in all areas of life, even identifying areas of unease in their bodies in order to heal. Additionally, Nami channels the archangels and spirit guides, translating their messages into beautiful colors on canvas. Many clients repeatedly return for painting sessions to see how they have progressed with their goals and how their guides suggest they move forward. Nami also clears houses and businesses, both in-person and remotely, to create a better energy flow.

Nami has painted more than 5,000 spiritual portraits and helped more than 10,000 clients. His deep and vast experience makes him an ideal healer, teacher, and mentor.

To find out more, visit: angelsbysunami.com.

To schedule a free fifteen-minute healing, reading, or clearing, mention "Clickety-Clack."

Nevaeh Pillsbury

How has the Clickety-Clack shown up in your life?

One of the most significant ways that the Clickety-Clack has presented itself in my life has been through my biological father. He was an abuser in many ways, of alcohol, of drugs, of himself, and of the people who surrounded him. I—for the first thirteen years of my life—got to experience him in all of his graces. My father was extremely mentally abusive and manipulative. As I was his child, I was given the opportunity to live through the way he used those skills in the worst ways.

One of the first things I can remember was looking up at my father and crying, as small children do when they need something. He looked back at me and told me, "I'm going to put you in a *choke hold!*"

This absolutely terrified me. I did not directly understand what he was saying, but I completely and clearly understood his malicious intent. That set the foundation for our father-daughter relationship. You can only imagine how much better it got.

I have numerous memories of my father's abuse, but the details aren't important. The bigger picture is that his constant manipulation, greed for power, drug use, and mental abuse of me and everyone in my family caused me to abandon my inner child. I reached a point where I was so overwhelmed by my emotions that I detached from any ability to feel anything that would make it harder to get through the day. I was in survival mode by the age of eleven.

I was put in a place where I was adopting the unhealthy habit of using distractions to ignore my problems. I was so overwhelmed by the details of my life that my body and mind unwillingly put me in a state of numbness to cope with the overwhelming amount of stress I was constantly under.

When I wasn't numb, suppressed emotions would surface—with no clarity on where they came from or what they meant—followed by a debilitating amount of loneliness. I had no one to guide me through any of what I was experiencing, which only made it all more confusing. I went through a lot of emotional turmoil, and all my unresolved emotions translated into an excessive amount of trauma.

At the time I was experiencing this trauma, my mother was working three jobs and still living paycheck to paycheck, as she was a young mother with four kids and her abusive husband didn't work. She served other people and shined light on the worst situations.

But raising a family by herself by working all the time with very little support, she lacked the time or energy to be there when my father's abuse took place. So those years I experienced this abuse and suppressed my inner child and inner truth was a time I experienced the Clickety-Clack.

How did you navigate the Clickety-Clack?

My process of navigating the Clickety-Clack began with healing my trauma. My childhood was normal to me, so I didn't understand at first that it caused trauma. Overcoming that was the best thing I've ever done for myself.

The beginning of that process looked and felt extremely bumpy. I felt out of place in myself. I was so disconnected from all parts of me that I had to teach myself to be vulnerable and truthful with myself. This was hard for me to do because I—like many others—was completely clueless about where to start.

I had the intention of finding a way to heal myself. I had no understanding of what manifestation even was when I made that intention. By framing the intention that I wanted to heal, I began manifesting the tools that would help me. One of the most significant tools I manifested—without realizing it—was yoga.

I began to practice yoga. At first, it was purely a physical practice for me as I didn't understand this was the tool that would propel my healing. Soon after I began, yoga became much more than a physical exercise. Soon, I decided to adopt the healthy habit of doing yoga every morning for my workout.

Slowly, I started to feel the way yoga affected me outside of my physical body. Yes, my muscles were gaining strength, and I could perform the postures that were once grueling with relative ease. But, I also felt the way my mind, body, and soul connected in the yoga postures. The interconnectedness I began to feel led me down the path of searching within myself and looking more toward Source for guidance and answers.

I was more open and, therefore, allowed whatever needed to come forth to do so. I began to process all the things I had experienced in the past without judgment of myself or the people around me when I was experiencing that trauma. I meditated and took time to understand myself and accepted that which was. Through all this, I learned with patience to identify the problems inside myself so I could move forward by letting go of the past.

I knew my childhood self never got an answer to the many questions she had, so I pulled all those questions out of me again in meditation. I worked on answering them so I could heal my inner child. I finally felt free from being held in the past by my unresolved trauma.

What tools do you recommend for staying peaceful in a seemingly toxic world?

There are a few things I do day to day that allow me to stay centered in neutrality within myself, no matter what might be happening around me.

One practice is doing some form of physical exercise. I've found this to be nourishing and calming to my physical and mental state. Moving my body has only good outcomes. It improves memory and brain function, lowers cortisol—the stress hormone—levels, protects against chronic diseases and pain, improves the quality of sleep, and can lengthen our overall lifespan. I try to implement exercise into my daily routine.

The practice of meditation is another method I use to remain peaceful. This might be different for me than for other people. For me, meditation means achieving a mentally clear and emotionally calm and stable state. I could reach that state through breathing practices, creating art, playing music, or practicing yoga. The consistency of reaching that place every day makes it easier for me to access a state of peace when I feel like I'm drifting from it.

Another tool that assists my ability to remain peaceful is something called *The Four Agreements*. Actively applying The Four Agreements to my life shifted my everyday interactions with people for the better. My feelings towards myself altered completely after reading the book, *The Four Agreements: A Practical Guide to Personal Freedom* by Don Miguel Ruiz (Amber-Allen Publishing, 1997). The code of conduct in the book allowed me to understand my internal state more clearly, and that understanding led to staying in a state of peace more easily. The Four Agreements are an amazing tool, and implementing them into my life has only made it easier.

One last thing: *Go stick your feet in some dirt.* Experience nature. It has so much to offer and asks for nothing in return. Go experience the stillness, the beauty, the direct connection to God, and the uninterrupted peace nature gives you. That will keep you peaceful in this seemingly toxic world.

About the Author

Nevaeh Pillsbury is the founder of an art business called BamArt (@bamArt.org) that features the meaningful and spiritual art she creates for those who are willing to expand their consciousness. Nevaeh is also a YouTuber who documents her journeys of traveling and experiencing the world through her eyes. Now she is an author, artist, business founder, and spiritual teacher, all at only seventeen years old.

If you would like to reach out to Nevaeh, visit her website at BamArt.org.

Contact her on:

    Instagram: @Nevaeh_things

    Facebook: @Nevaeh Pillsbury

    YouTube: Nevaeh Travels and shares all her adventures

Lisa Jeanine Ramirez

How has the Clickety-Clack shown up in your life?

I had some solid dreams growing up. For instance, when I was nine years old, I knew I was going to become an optometrist. I manifested that. Becoming a mom was another dream I had.

The Clickety-Clack showed up in my life when I did not have a clear and solid dream—something positive I was working toward. I **believed** I did not need a **man** in my life. So when I got pregnant, my Clickety-Clack began. When I became a mom, I saw how hard it was to be a single mom and to have a co-parenting relationship. I couldn't figure it out, so I really struggled.

After becoming a mom, I quickly experienced how hard it was to be a single mom while trying to raise a child with a person who completely disrespected and bullied me. It made me feel unsafe. I tried to find a sense of protection and respect outside myself through the legal system, lawyers, judges, police, and boyfriends. I basically searched everywhere except for the one place where I eventually found it.

All these efforts just kept me in the Clickety-Clack, because at the end of the day, I was not trusting myself or my intuition. I was not loving myself, feeling worthy, or giving myself the respect I deserved. I wasn't trusting my intuition; therefore, I was not able to tap into my divinity as I was trying to find answers from outside sources.

I didn't realize at the time the security and respect I was searching for lay within me. As I learned to love myself, trust myself, and respect myself, I followed my inner-guidance system. I learned I am the only one who can control my actions and behaviors in order to always feel loved, respected, and protected. I have no control over the actions of others, and if I am the only one who controls my thoughts and behaviors, then how I care for and love myself is everything.

How did you navigate the Clickety-Clack?

I navigated the Clickety-Clack by finding things that helped me little by little. I gravitated toward tools that helped me love myself, know myself, and gain a sense of who I was inside. I found yoga. I found meditation. I found different pieces of the puzzle that were the exact pieces I needed.

I have always believed that outside sources, even though they may not lead to the answers, are part of the process. We all go through a learning process. Nobody can tell you the right way for you—except you. When you look for outside sources, they can provide ideas and possibilities, but no one can solve what you are trying to solve except *you.*

But we still do need to learn through these other sources. I navigated through numerous lawyers. I navigated through working on myself, trusting myself, loving myself. I learned lessons from my kids, and I learned from my co-parents. I learned to set boundaries, and I learned to love and respect myself. Little by little is how I did it.

What tools do you recommend for staying peaceful in a seemingly toxic world?

The tools that I recommend for staying peaceful in a seemingly toxic world are truly loving yourself and knowing yourself. It seems easy, to love yourself. You may think: *Oh, I am going to get a manicure and get my hair done*, and that is loving yourself. However, truly loving yourself means loving all parts of you.

We all have our shadows—we have our good points and our bad points. We need to be able to love all those parts, to really accept and know ourselves.

You are like an onion. You can peel an onion, but there are some layers that seem to refuse to peel back. Those layers take a little more time and a little more love. Love is the answer. Loving *yourself* is the answer. If you do not love yourself, how can you love anyone else?

In this world, we are used to conditional love. Nothing feels worse than love with conditions.

One thing that has helped me a lot is *Dream Weaving*. It's a living workshop, and it has helped me to truly experience unconditional love. In experiencing this unconditional love from others, I have learned to love myself. Unconditional love is a never-ending process that can heal anything.

Loving yourself, no matter what, will shift you out of the Clickety-Clack as quickly as possible. Loving myself unconditionally has made me bold and brave. On Instagram, I've been doing some fun and crazy things, such as dancing and posting without pre-planning every second of my post. I'm becoming comfortable in front of the camera, and the freedom I am feeling has helped me love myself even more.

About the Author

Lisa Jeanine Ramirez is the principal owner of Angel Eye Care. She is a Tulane University graduate with a Bachelor of Science degree in Ecology, Evolution, and Organismal Biology, and a minor in Spanish (*Sí, yo hablo español*).

She also graduated from The Inter-American University of Puerto Rico with her Doctorate of Optometry and is certified by the National Board of Examiners in Optometry in the Treatment and Management of Ocular Disease.

Lisa has spent the last twenty years practicing her passion for the eyes and being the mother of two amazing souls, Lukas and Nicolas Mar, who have definitely taught her the most important lessons of her life—far greater than any degree she has earned.

The Universe continues to amaze and affirm that she is on the right path, discovering her purpose more and more each day.

For more information, you can email Lisa at:
angeleyecare@yahoo.com.

Or visit:

Instagram: @chakracolada

Facebook: Lisa Jeanine Ramirez

Private Group: Chakra Colada

Dipal Shah

How has the Clickety-Clack shown up in your life?

In my life, the Clickety-Clack has shown up in many ways, but specifically, it showed up in my move from pharmaceuticals to being a holistic practitioner of energy medicine. I never thought I would take that route. I always wanted to be in pharmaceuticals. It was my dream job, but life took a one-eighty when I started looking for my own health solutions.

For a time, I was quite ambitious in the pharmaceutical industry. I wanted to be a manager; I wanted to lead a team; I wanted to make an impact not only in the company but also in the lives of millions of people. The only way I knew was through Western medicine, even though my background is all in Eastern medicine, as I grew up in the Hindu culture. I never really learned Eastern medicine until later when I went into holistic practice.

That moment of leaving my job, finding a new purpose after two years, and becoming an energy medicine practitioner—that is when the Clickety-Clack moment happened in my life. It is beautiful to now see how it unfolded so naturally. At first, there was a huge sense of uncertainty about what was going to happen in my life, but I knew I was always taken care of by the Universe, and that ultimately led me to where I am today.

How did you navigate the Clickety-Clack?

There are always turning points that lead us to our purpose in life, and it is interesting how they show up after a certain age. For me, the turning point showed up in my late thirties to now forties.

I navigated the Clickety-Clack by taking time for myself. I left my job. Of course, I was scared to leave my job because I had been working ever since I was seventeen, and it was in the time of the downturn. We needed the money; however, we also knew it would be okay if I left my job.

I left my position as a pharmaceutical sales rep. Just before I left, I had held one of the highest positions in the company. I knew I wanted to be a mom and stay home to care for my children when they were young; I just did not know how long I would be a stay-at-home mom.

I took time to give myself the self-care I needed. I went to chiropractors and found natural complementary medicines to help my body recover from the illness it was carrying. I was having digestive problems that left me in pain most of the time— GERD, gallbladder pain, leaky gut, constipation, ulcers, and kidney stones. I quit because I was tired of traveling and didn't have time for myself or the kids. I was bored and wanted to do something different with my life.

I didn't feel as though I had cancer or anything fatal; however, I experienced a lot of emotional and physical discomfort. I was not happy because I could not live my daily life. I was constantly filling my cabinets with supplements and medications and seeking out a doctor who could help me.

I soon realized I needed to do more inner work rather than looking outward for a resolution for my health. Once I focused on the inner work, I began doing things I love, such as dancing, spending time in nature, meditating, and yoga. I did more and more for myself—something I had never done before.

As I started to do more self-care, my body started to heal. Peace of mind came into play. Then I started to manifest what I wanted in my life. Ultimately, I found my purpose.

What tools do you recommend for staying peaceful in a seemingly toxic world?

The number one tool I recommend is self-care. And I don't mean going to get a massage occasionally or finally going on that much-needed vacation. Those activities are not self-care. Self-care should happen every day as soon as you awaken. Wake up with a smile on your face, knowing that you are alive and get to make a difference somewhere. Self-care comes from going within, recognizing your emotions—what you're holding onto and what you can let go.

The second tool I recommend is to know that you are limitless. When you know that you are limitless, you let go of the fear and the doubts that hold you back from doing anything and everything you want to do.

Everyone says: *Oh, I do not have time, or, Oh, I can't do this. I don't know how.*

Trust me, you can do anything. All you need is to know you are limitless. When you put your mind to something, all you need to do is say, *Yes, I can,* and things will simply unfold. Once you fully trust that you are limitless, the right people will show up for you, the right circumstances will occur, and the right doors will open for you. That is what happened to me.

The third tool I recommend is harnessing your true power. There are times as children when we lost our power. The same is true as adults and as teens. We have all been in circumstances and situations where it seems we have lost power, but then we found our resilience and our way of connecting with who we are—the truth of our own power.

We need to stick with it. We cannot let someone or something take away our power. We have a beautiful light within us that illuminates every part of our being. If we can keep our connection to that light within, we will always know we have this superpower within us. And we will stand strong in that power when someone or something tries to tell us anything different.

About the Author

Dipal Shah is an internationally acclaimed medical intuitive and self-care expert, global speaker, and spiritual mentor celebrated by clients across the globe who refer to her as "The Body Whisperer." As a recognized expert in the field of energy medicine, Dipal is the creator of the *Quantum Body Awakening Technique*. Her globally taught course teaches empaths over forty how to become the master of their own health and well-being.

Dipal has helped thousands in over ninety-two countries break free from chronic health problems in conjunction with or where western medicine has failed. By identifying the root cause of their symptoms, Dipal has helped her clients create powerful and profound shifts inside and out, allowing them to find more joy and inspiration in all aspects of their lives. Dipal has worked with celebrities, healthcare practitioners, thought leaders, and many others.

She has been featured in top media outlets, such as ABC, NBC, Fox, CBS, and in telesummits around the world. She is a writer for *Best Holistic Life Magazine.* Her mission is to provide a wealth of Eastern knowledge along with her intuitive gifts to help people heal naturally.

Grab your *free* "Daily Empowerment" and "Self-Love Meditation" for a quick boost for the day: ananda4life.ac-page. com/SelfLoveMeditation.

Jenny Stapleton

How has the Clickety-Clack shown up in your life?

The Clickety-Clack has shown up in various ways throughout my life.

In 1995, there was an earthquake in Japan that shook up my life. I realized then that material things don't really matter, and I started to go with the flow a little bit more. As I stepped into this newfound flow, I applied for job after job and was told repeatedly that I was *not a fit*. Working with and for others did not prove to be an enjoyable experience for me in the long term, though I did put in a lot of effort and often burned myself out at work.

In 2015, my husband suffered a spinal cord injury. It changed the course of our lives and my self-care. Additionally, my mother, Shoshanna, became sick with congestive heart failure, and she asked me to be her power of attorney. Becoming a caregiver to my loved ones shocked my nervous system, yet also filled my cup. It surprisingly used all of my transferable skills from work and fit my personality much more than my paying jobs did.

How did you navigate the Clickety-Clack?

While I have recently transitioned from being a teacher and employee to becoming an entrepreneur, I come from a family that desired me to have a secured job. However, once the Clickety-Clack started shaking things up for my husband and me, I felt called to support not only the two of us but many others as well. I started thinking new thoughts and making new choices, which included my decision to go back to school, focusing on grief, loss, and bereavement to help people with the hardest time of their lives—as well as help other caregivers.

When my mother Shoshanna grew sick with congestive heart failure and asked me to be her power of attorney (POA), she lived in California and I lived in Canada. Even though my husband had a spinal cord injury at that time, I was able to take care of the many duties the responsibility of being a POA entailed. I was able to make sure she received the very best care, and I helped get her affairs in order.

I did not have a lot of support during that time, so I would listen for guidance. I decided to help others going through unpredictable circumstances and seeking guidance in the same way I did.

I also navigated the Clickety-Clack when I discovered a book, called *The Power*, in *The Secret* series by Rhonda Byrne, and it guided me to a different way of looking at my bills. I also learned how to manage my money. Even if I only had a hundred dollars, I would manage it better while always paying myself a little bit, giving a little bit, and following the *jar system*. If you have ever heard of T. Harv Eker, you've heard of the jar system. I read his books, and they taught me to look at money differently.

I learned that I am in control of what I have, and I learned to appreciate what I have. I did not have a lot of money. I learned that when I was a caregiver, I was a lot more affluent in time. I was volunteering a lot, and I was working a lot. I was the one who would burn the candle on both ends. I was up early, would get to the job on time, would stay late, and would finish it. I was a project-based person. But I really did not have a lot of time to spend at home with my husband and my dogs, until I became a caregiver.

I've come to realize that I have love abundance with my husband, and I have experienced time abundance. I have a lot of abundance in my life in other ways. I am truly grateful, even as an entrepreneur starting out.

The Clickety-Clack showed up because of the circumstances, and I learned not to worry as much along the way. I changed some of my values, such as traveling. My husband and I used to love to travel. I still want to travel with him at some point, but that is currently not my number one value.

I have found ways to practice self-care: taking ten minutes here and there for breath work, taking time for meditation using calm.com and other meditation tools, going to a movie for two hours, or pushing the envelope by going to a play in another city for four hours. When I expanded into giving myself self-care, it was very satisfying.

What tools do you recommend for staying peaceful in a seemingly toxic world?

Three tools I recommend are PQ (Positive Intelligence Quotient) Reps, music, and guided meditations.

I am currently learning about positive intelligence. Positive intelligence is reconnecting with a sage person within you—realizing that everything you are looking for *outside* yourself is actually *inside* you. In a story related to what I am learning, a Golden Buddha in Thailand was once covered with mud and clay, to protect it during a war. People had forgotten about it over time. One day, a monk started chipping away at the mud and clay and was ridiculed for wasting his time and energy. He continued chipping away at it until the beautiful Golden Buddha was revealed.

What I take from this story is that every single person on this Earth has a Golden Buddha inside them, so it's very important to not give up when they are chipping away at the layers of gunk on their life journey. Fulfillment and freedom come from re-discovering the essence of the person we are born to be.

Positive intelligence is uncovering your true self—the self you can see in your childhood photos, for example. I learned this while completing a lot of photo projects during COVID, and I reconnected to the essence of me that is innocent and full of love, light, and levity. I would say that my daily "Positive Quotient" or PQ Repetitions practice is one of the best tools I use so far for navigating the daily Clickety-Clack noise, keeping my focus more on what I love and less on what's annoying me.

Regarding music, I was a music major, and when I played for myself, there was a lot of love. I loved sitting at the piano, playing what was written or playing by ear. Music provides a way to express yourself that words or physicality cannot touch. I have been listening to music a lot more recently, as well. During COVID, I practiced self-care by going to concerts online and virtually touring museums I enjoy, such as Museum London, the

Van Gogh Museum, the Louvre, and other venues that allow us to experience art and connect on the web. Therefore, I found different ways to connect with adventure and entertainment, which I highly value.

Calm.com has been a great tool for my own meditation practice. It helped me sleep, focus, breathe better and be less anxious. I recommend that you honor your breath, especially if you are a caregiver. If you pay attention to your breath, you may notice sometimes it's really shallow—you won't hear it or feel it at first, until you start paying attention to it. Take a moment right now, to sense your breath and all it includes: the inhale, the exhale, and the temperature; try putting your finger under your nose and feeling the temperature of the air that goes in and out. This exercise can ground you quickly. Being grounded helps you live a much more satisfying life, and it all starts with the quality of your breath.

About the Author

A graduate from King's University College with a certificate in Loss, Grief, and Bereavement studies, Jenny has supported caregivers and palliative care nurses at WeCare Home Health Services and hospitals as a volunteer and has organized wellness programs at hospices. She is also a licensed Willow End-of-Life educator, a certified transformation facilitator, and an award-winning international bestselling author.

Jenny Stapleton aims to support caregivers as they move through the sudden changes and transitions in caregiving. She addresses the burnout, isolation, and overwhelm that often accompany long-term care. Working with Jenny, caregivers gain a new perspective on what matters most in life and are supported in their efforts to care for themselves so that they are able to better care for others.

Jenny's passion is bringing caregivers fun, freedom, and fulfillment, even if they don't personally believe it's possible. She believes that living an empowered life is possible, even as a caregiver.

Contact Jenny Stapleton, your Caregiver Coach. Find out more by visiting: GuidingByYourSide.com.

$\mathcal{DL}$ $\mathcal{W}alker$

How has the Clickety-Clack shown up in your life?

If you ever get the opportunity to meet me, you might look at me and think I am a healthy, happy, and vibrant person. Usually, I am. Helping people be healthy is my passion and my career, and it is definitely my life's calling. As a result, I have not only been blessed with great health, but have a knack for helping others overcome their serious health-related challenges.

I have had to face such challenges in my own life a couple of times as well. Back in 2011, I was that patient. I was a victim of a medical error that was an undiagnosed sterile infection after a routine dental implant surgery—very, very, very rare. After I discontinued my post-surgical antibiotics, I began feeling pain in my jaw that progressively became worse. I have a pretty high threshold to pain, but this pain was different. It was intractable! I could not get comfortable. There was nothing I could do to get rid of it. So, I shifted into my diagnostic detective mode, put the pieces of the health puzzle together, and knew with certainty that I had an infection.

When I contacted my surgeon, he said, "Nope, it is impossible that you have an infection with a dental implant." He took X-rays that showed nothing, suggested my pain was allergies, and gave me a prescription for pain medication, which I knew I was not going to take.

I know that the brain can create pain, so I asked myself: *Is this really in my head?* and the answer was *no*. In the past, I was able to overcome health challenges quickly, but not this time. In physical therapy school, I was taught very little about teeth. Honestly, I knew nothing about dentistry.

I understood firsthand what it was like to be many of my patients—dismissed by the person trained to help when you feel as if something is wrong with you. My daughter was four at the time, and I remember walking her in her stroller, petrified at the possibility that I would never be able to care for her in the way I was used to or be the mom she deserved. For the first and only time in my life, I was concerned not only about my future, but also my future life.

How did you navigate the Clickety-Clack?

First, I believed in myself, and I was determined to figure out the root cause of this problem just like I did and still do for many of my clients. I then did exactly what I tell my clients to do: First of all, know and believe that your answer is out there. Keep going until you find it. Do not ever give up.

Two, find the people who believe in you and are going to help you. Do not spend your time on those that are not. Just say, *thank you very much*, and move on.

Three, be polite but not a pushover. Step on some toes if you need to. I went over this doctor's head and called an infectious disease practice. He was not too happy about it. But if a person is not helping you, find someone who can and move on as quickly as possible. Do not waste your time.

For this situation, I did my own physical therapy evaluation of myself. I found and consulted an endodontist, a maxillofacial (oral maxillary) surgeon, a dental school professor, my family doctor, my physical therapy colleagues, Dr. Google (of course), and then, eventually, I went back to my surgeon. He then did something he had never done before—he opened up my stitches and discovered my infection.

The problem was resolved completely in about three weeks. My surgeon provided the proper diagnosis and the course of treatment and let me know that he learned something from this experience. So did I. What I learned is that health is our most precious thing, our most precious asset. It affects not only you but the people in your life.

I now know what it is like to live with chronic pain; you are a shadow of your true self. Chronic pain affects all the relationships in your life, especially the one with yourself. And what I know for certain is that the outcome would have been very different if I did not know what I know and the people I know. Most people do not have the benefit of my knowledge and training.

This experience is why I have dedicated my career to teaching people how to heal and take control of their healthcare, sharing all my knowledge and healing power with them. I help others realize their own power and potential to heal and recover.

What tools do you recommend for staying peaceful in a seemingly toxic world?

I have the four Rs. First you must *realize* something is wrong. Then you need to *research* and *recognize* the *root cause*. What is this really about? It could be body, mind, or energy.

Pain is your body's way of telling you that something is wrong in any shape, way, or form—physical, emotional, or spiritual. It is up to you to figure out the message. Then, you need to respond with a body, mind, energy approach. You need to address all three because those are your keys to unlock the mystery.

I throw every resource I have at a particular resolution when I am trying to calm myself in my body. I often combine breathwork with a visualization or a mantra. When you breathe in, it's what you are inspiring or inhaling into your life. Then your exhale is called expiration, which is like death. You exhale what you are putting to death that no longer serves you with the movement of your rib cage, your diaphragm, and your body.

Finally, I love re-stabilization frequencies, and I play them on a frequency generator. The specific frequencies I love playing are 528 Hz, 432 Hz, and 122–26 Hz.

My final go-to is gratitude. Whenever I am feeling like complete and utter crap about a situation or something that is going on in my life, I shift into gratitude. Specifically, I practice three minutes of gratitude: one minute of gratitude for something in the past, one minute for what I am grateful for in the present, and one minute for the future. I realize that in any moment what is going on is going on, and I can choose to be happy or sad about it. It's my choice and I am in control.

About the Author

DL Walker is a healer, teacher, and diagnostic detective whose wellness approach includes body, mind, and energy. Her formal education includes two Bachelor of Science degrees in Fitness/Cardiac Rehab and Physical Therapy, respectively, and a Master of Science degree in Exercise Science. A lifelong learner, DL has completed advanced certifications in Functional Manual Therapy, Health Coaching, and Energetic Medicine. Sharing what she has learned over her thirty-five years in wellness, healthcare, and rehabilitation, she has dedicated her life and career to returning the power of healing back to individuals.

DL's passion is determining the root causes of clinical symptoms, which she terms *diagnostic detecting*. She then creates comprehensive mind, body, and energy solution strategies that *guide* people through a process not only to undo existing symptomatology but to optimize lasting results in the fastest way possible.

Her online membership program, called Correcticise™, teaches recovery and restorative activities to people in their forties and beyond for their body, mind, and energy, so they are empowered to live a life without limits and are unstoppable at any age.

Currently, DL keeps busy learning and developing new healing strategies, honing her clinical skills, teaching, coaching, consulting, and creating courses with the intention of helping the people of the world heal from sole to soul.

Contact DL on her website: dlwalkerconsultant.com.

Be guided through these techniques and reclaim your healing power with DL's Correcticise membership. Discover hundreds of instructional videos to optimize health, as well as fully recover from injury through and with body, mind, and energy activities. Access Correcticise free for seven days at https://www.fixuonline.com/correcticise. Take back complete control of your healing and wellness so you can live your best life now and in your fabulous future.

Renee Zukin

How has the Clickety-Clack shown up in your life?

Our lives are often defined by the big transitions, but how we move through them is what makes us who we are. Each new experience of the Clickety-Clack gives us an opportunity to learn more about ourselves and our place in this world—who we are, who we want to become, and with whom we are here to create meaningful connections.

One of the most profound transitional times in my life took place between 2007 and 2009. I was in the midst of a divorce and raising three young children at home, I had just changed jobs, I was moving out of the classroom and into educational publishing, and I was newly diagnosed with obsessive-compulsive disorder (OCD). Talk about shifting gears!

My therapist at the time suggested I begin journaling a few times a week, something I had done pretty regularly in my teens and early twenties—before kids, work, and other adulting tasks that tend to pull our attention away from ourselves. My pen took to paper like nothing before, and I instinctively knew that writing was going to be how I would find my way through.

What I couldn't predict then was just how transforming writing and connecting to the creative process would be, and I'm grateful to now understand that prioritizing creative expression in all forms is healing and vital to experiencing life to the fullest.

How did you navigate the Clickety-Clack?

The work to heal and thrive—despite grieving the loss of my marriage and navigating a newer, rockier terrain of anxiety and OCD—was multifaceted. I worked regularly with a therapist, understanding how the experiences of my past may have still been affecting my present.

I read books that helped me change my perspective on what was happening around and within me, like *Conscious Living* by Gay Hendricks and *The Seat of the Soul* by Gary Zukav. I took diligent notes in my journal so I could use what I was learning about the power of my choices and beliefs to make significant changes to release old patterns and take the reins in my life. And, most importantly, I wrote.

Poems, songs, stories, and more came pouring out of me onto the notebook. On some nights, when my former husband had the kids, I would take myself on dates to listen to jazz at the Sanctuary Bar, a small, darkened room with fancy beers on tap and the best gourmet pizza in town. I'd pull out my notebook, letting the rhythmic sounds and phrases pass through me while my pen told stories of its own on the page.

Giving myself the time and space to create allowed for more time and space to open up, as I could once again feel truly present in my body. This allowed me to be more present and mindful with my children and my work and provided a new understanding of my place in relationship to others.

Writing allowed me to experience a bird's eye view of my life, and that distance cultivated more self-compassion and grace for what I was going through, rather than beating myself up about mistakes I thought I'd made. It allowed me to grow and shift into new ways of relating with the world that offered a supportive gaze and ignited empowered, inspired action.

Was I still fearful at times about the impact my decisions to get divorced and change jobs would have on my life and those around me? Yes.

Was I still worried about how long and difficult a road it would be to navigate the therapies that would work to ease the symptoms of OCD? Yep.

But granting myself permission to begin writing brought me so much joy in the midst of it all. Creative expression was the glue that held me together. It was the *Light* at the end of a dark tunnel that showed me there was, indeed, a way out and that life wasn't always going to feel so hard.

As the different pieces of writing continued to flow, I thought about putting together a collection of poems and essays for publication. With my new job, I was learning all about the different processes involved in publishing that could easily be transferred from the educational market to mainstream literature. However, much of what was coming through—inspired by relationships and experiences in my life that helped shape who I was at the time—were songs.

I'd write a poem, but melodies came along with it. I found myself humming in my cubicle as I worked. When I'd get home later, I began building musical structures and expanding the poems into lyrics. I dug deeper into the process and began spending more time out in the world listening to music, connecting with musicians, and seeing clearly how linked music and emotions are.

We can experience a wide range of moods and healing through song, and this was where my heart soared. I wrote songs about healing and moving through fear, songs about connection and the mystery of love, songs about reclaiming one's own power and finding a sense of self-redemption. The experience cracked me open, and I was forever changed—truly understanding how making the space for creation allowed everything else in life to flow with more ease and beauty.

As a kid, I'd always dreamed of performing in a band. I sang in choir in high school, but never had the opportunity to really *rock out* on stage like some of my idols: Joan Jett, Madonna, or Jim Morrison of The Doors. One of the things that writing helped me find again was that passion to sing and perform.

While I wasn't going to be the next Carole King or Lady Gaga, I did understand that I could curate this dream in small ways. I found amazing local musicians who heard my melodies and lyrics and wanted to be part of the process of building a musical foundation. We formed a band and began playing regular gigs in bars, coffee shops, and the farmer's market. We played together for a couple of years and ultimately decided to record an album. The album, *Sense of Redemption*, was filled with the songs I had written to heal my heart, and as I spoke and wrote openly about the process of bringing the music to life, it allowed others to experience their own challenges from a new perspective.

In those days, blogs were big. It seemed like everyone had one, and I wrote frequently about my struggles with anxiety, OCD, relationships, and creative flow. It was here that others began finding solace and inspiration to go within and find ways to express themselves in order to navigate anxieties, transitions, and challenges.

Through the years since, I have turned to writing time and again to make sense of the world. I even returned to the classroom and had better tools to support my students in finding their own voices and navigating the tumultuous times of teenage angst. I continued to study multiple psychological and healing modalities to support others on the journey, and now I lead workshops and hold space for individuals doing their inner work to see outer change.

Who knew that some of the hardest times in my life would bring about the most magnificent gifts?

The Clickety-Clack may be loud and challenging, but if we keep pedaling and find a way to enjoy the wind on our face and the warmth of the sun just beyond the clouds as we push ourselves to the next level, we will find peace.

What tools do you recommend for staying peaceful in a seemingly toxic world?

Find what lights you up. If you don't even know what that might be, find someone to help you see through the murky waters—a therapist, a coach, a healer, a guide.

Create. For the sake of pure joy and expression. Draw, sing, dance, build, write, for *you*, not for an end game or for producing something *worthy*. Though, you will find that the more you create, those things can come, too, if you desire them.

Take time to listen within and communicate openly with yourself and others.

Be in nature, in stillness, and gaze upon your surroundings with wonder.

Practice self-compassion as you navigate challenges; replace judgment with curiosity.

When you are stuck in overwhelm, just do the very next step, and then the next. My mom always used to tell me, "How do you eat an elephant? One bite as a time."

Hug more. Fight less.

Know that nothing lasts forever, and this, too, shall pass. Even if the situation is unchangeable, your perspective and responses are not.

Be brave, every day.

About the Author

Renee Zukin is a writer and educator who uses creative expression as a tool for reconnecting to one's inner wisdom, supporting heart-centered entrepreneurs to create magnetic marketing copy in order to cultivate more impact and income with their message, as well as helping people navigate life's transitions to heal through writing.

With more than twenty years of experience as a writer, editor, and teacher, as well as studying multiple psychological and healing modalities, Renee created the *Rebel Writers Community and Workshops* to provide a space for others to use the written word as a tool for self-healing and empowerment.

Through her own writing, music, and mentorship, she has helped people reclaim their authentic voice to communicate their transformational message—sending a ripple effect of evolution, expansion, and elevation around the globe.

Renee earned her Bachelor of Arts in Language and Literature from the University of Michigan and her Master of Arts in Teaching from the University of Iowa. She is a certified teacher, trained in Mindfulness for Educators, Restorative Justice, and Community Circles. Additionally, she holds a Reiki II certification and is a lifelong learner of personal growth, psychology, energy medicine, and living consciously.

If you've been thinking about journaling or writing or want to try either for the first time, download her free guide to "Jumpstart Your Journal" and tune in to your inner wisdom and creative flow to help navigate life's challenges: www.reneezukin.com/journal.

Conclusion

As you reach the end of this book, our hope as the publishers is that you are inspired by the incredible people we have invited to share insights, stories, tips, and tools for navigating the Clickety-Clack of life and staying peaceful within, even when things around you are seemingly toxic.

You may notice we use the word *seemingly* in front of the word *toxic*. This is for a specific purpose. Many of our authors love the world and are able to accept whatever is happening around them, still seeing the world as good. Because they use the tools they share with you, they are either unphased by outward appearances, or in many cases, the time they stay in the negative passes quickly. Seeing the world as toxic is ultimately a choice: One can look at the same event and see it as toxic, or a challenge, a learning experience, or, as some say, "It is what it is." It's all perspective.

As you read our authors' answers to the three questions, do you feel connected to any of them or their perspectives?

If you connect to any of our contributors in strong and meaningful ways, we suggest you reach out to them. Look up the people, websites, programs, or products they mentioned within their chapter of the book.

Our wish for you—like those we have invited to be in this book—is to be a walking, talking demonstration of being able to stay neutral, calm, and peaceful, no matter what is happening in the outside world.

Thank you for reading this book!

Keith Leon S.

Multiple International Award-Winning Author, Speaker, and Publisher

LeonSmithPublishing.com

BeyondBeliefPublishing.com

About the Publisher

In 2004, Babypie Publishing was founded by entrepreneurs Keith and Maura Leon when they decided to self-publish their co-authored book, *The Seven Steps to Successful Relationships*. When Babypie published its second book a few years later— Keith Leon's *Who Do You Think You Are? Discover the Purpose of Your Life*, implementing a large marketing campaign that introduced the book to over a million people on the first day it came out—both books became bestsellers overnight.

After the success of their first two titles, Keith and Maura were approached by another author who believed they could take his book to bestseller status as well. They decided to give it a shot, and Warren Henningsen's book, *If I Can You Can: Insights of an Average Man*, became an international bestseller the day it was released.

Before long, Babypie Publishing was receiving manuscript submissions from all over the world and publishing such titles as Ronny K. Prasad's *Welcome to Your Life*; Melanie Eatherton's *The 7-Minute Mirror*; and Maribel Jimenez and Keith Leon's *The*

Bake Your Book Program: How to Finish Your Book Fast and Serve It Up HOT!

With a vision to make an even greater impact, Babypie Publishing began offering comprehensive writing and publishing programs, as well as a full range of à la carte services to support independent authors and innovative professionals in getting their message out in the most powerful and effective manner. In 2015, Keith and Maura developed the YouSpeakIt Book Program to make it easy, fast, and affordable for busy entrepreneurs and cutting-edge health practitioners to share their mission and message with the world.

In 2016, Leon Smith Publishing was created as the new home for Babypie, YouSpeakIt, and future projects. In 2018, Beyond Belief Publishing was added as an imprint for spiritual and esoteric titles.

Keith Leon S. has continued to write books, speak, and teach on stages worldwide, and he mentors authors in the easiest, most effective ways to market their mission, message, and books. Keith is a five-time award-winning, seven-time International Bestselling Author who has spoken at events that included Jack Canfield, Bob Proctor, Dr. John Demartini, Neale Donald Walsch, Barbara De Angelis, Dr. John Gray, Dr. Michael Beckwith, Bob Doyle, Marci Shimoff, Joe Vitale, Marie Diamond, and Marianne Williamson.

Keith has appeared on many popular radio and television broadcasts on ABC, CBS, NBC, and The Jenny McCarthy Show, to name just a few, and his work has been covered by *Inc.* magazine, *LA Weekly*, *The Huffington Post*, and *Succeed Magazine*.

Whether you're a transformational author looking for writing and publishing services or a visionary leader ready to take your life and work to the next level, we thank you for visiting our website at LeonSmithPublishing.com, and we look forward to serving you.

Made in the USA
Monee, IL
21 February 2023